Cast-Iron Cooking

$12.95

Cookbooks by A. D. Livingston

OUTDOOR LIFE'S COMPLETE FISH & GAME COOKBOOK
GOOD VITTLES
CAST IRON COOKING

Other Books by A. D. Livingston

THE SKY'S THE LIMIT, A NOVEL
POKER STRATEGY AND WINNING PLAY
DEALING WITH CHEATS
FISHING FOR BASS
ADVANCED BASS TACKLE AND BOATS
FLY-RODDING FOR BASS
TYING BASS FLIES AND BUGS

Cast-Iron

COOKING

from Johnnycakes

to

Blackened Redfish

A. D. Livingston

LYONS & BURFORD, PUBLISHERS

for Ike

Printed in the United States of America

10 9 8 7 6 5 4 3 2 1

Illustrations by Richard Harrington

Library of Congress Cataloging-in-Publication Data

Livingston, A. D., 1932-
   Cast-iron cooking : from johnnycakes to blackened redfish / A.D.
   Livingston.
         p.   cm.
   Includes index.
   ISBN (invalid) 15582211101
   1. Skillet cookery.   I. Title.
   TX840.S55L58   1991
641.7′7—dc20   90-23115
                                                         CIP

Contents

That Ol' Black Magic

As anyone who's simmered a pot of catfish stew by a riverbank can tell you, a well-seasoned iron pot or skillet is impossible to beat for creating exotic flavors in many home-cooked meals. Where other cookware strives to leave no taste in food, the iron pot, when properly seasoned, will instill a distinctive flavor that becomes richer as the seasoning ages over many years of use.

—*The South Carolina Wildlife Cookbook*

A Manly Tradition

I hide my favorite frying pan whenever my mother-in-law comes for a visit. This good arm-and-hammer woman doesn't merely wash the dishes, singing and humming and enjoying the soap suds as she goes. She grits her teeth shut as she scrubs and scours, and within 30 minutes she can make even a well-blackened pot or pan look downright spic and span. The woman means well, but, of course, scrubbing a cast-iron skillet is wellnigh (but not quite) the worst thing that you can do to it.

I have the opposite problem with my good wife. A modern woman, she doesn't scrub anything. Instead, she merely stuffs pots and pans into the dishwasher along with the dishes and silverware—which is, to be sure, even worse than scrubbing cast-iron ware. Even well-seasoned skillets and Dutch ovens go into the machine, sometimes piled on

*The skillet or frying pan is the most popular piece
of modern cast-iron cookware.*

top of everything else. Or under everything else. Whatever doesn't come out clean simply gets another cycle or two. Of course, everything stays in the steamy machine until the next washing. Although I allow that dishwashers with convenient pull-out racks are quite handy for storing glassware, be warned that cast iron ought to be stored bone dry, as will be discussed a little later.

One of my sons doesn't wash anything, with or without mechanical aid, and he can somehow mess up a non-stick surface of a cast-iron skillet while merely scrambling half a dozen chicken eggs for a light breakfast. Then he leaves the mess on a hot stove to harden. The boy shows a talent for cooking, and, for that reason, I try not to fuss at him. But maybe the time has come for him to get his own skillet. He will, I'm sure, start off with Teflon. After wearing out several dozen of these, at considerable expense, he will come to his senses, and, remembering his father's smother-fried round steak, he will discover the wisdom of the old ways. Cast-iron cooking is an American tradition, started no doubt at hearthside by the colonial goodwives and spread across the country by the brave, hardy women who followed the pioneers westward. But, alas, it's a tradition that must be carried on by us menfolks. Recall the mountain man, the '49er, the cowboy, and, perhaps, the firemen of Nantucket.

UNDERSTANDING CAST IRON

After iron ore has been smelted in a blast furnace, the immediate product is called pig iron. It can be refined further into wrought iron or steel, or it can be cast into pots, vats, Dutch ovens, and so on, in which case it is called cast iron.

Unlike steel, cast iron has no great tensile strength and it tends to be somewhat brittle. Nor can it be easily forged. But it is easy to sand cast, and it happens to withstand high temperatures. Thus, it is ideal for use in cookware that is used on red hot coals in a fireplace or at a campsite. Further, cast iron is a rather porous material, and it will take what is called a seasoning or "sweetening." In short, it more or less absorbs oil, which, in cooking, forms a protective coating on the surface, so that a drop of water will dance on it. Cast iron is the original no-stick material, and it lasts until the "sweetening" is lost by mistreatment. Sweetening and caring for cast-iron cookware is discussed a few paragraphs below.

Moreover, cast-iron cookware heats evenly and holds heat for a long time, as compared to aluminum. Partly because of its thickness, cast-iron cookware isn't as likely to have hotspots, and it isn't as likely to burn food on the bottom.

One disadvantage is that cast-iron cookware is quite heavy, partly because thin pieces would be more difficult to sand cast. A 12-inch skillet, for example, weighs 7 pounds, and an 8-quart Dutch oven with lid weighs 16 pounds. Clearly, this stuff isn't for the backpacker, although it might be a purely excellent choice for a remote camp, simply because it is very versatile, quite durable, and will cook everything from sourdough bread to beaver stew.

Another disadvantage is that a cast-iron piece will sometimes crack if it is heated fast and unevenly. For this reason, large cast-iron vats and wash pots are usually partly filled with water or lard before they are heated. Cracking usually isn't a problem, however, with the smaller pieces. Most cast-iron cookware can be put directly onto a hot bed of campfire coals without a problem. It won't warp like lighter cookware. Further, cast iron is the only cookware that withstands, time after time, the heat required for the relatively new "blackened redfish" kind of cooking.

TENDER LOVING CARE

Because I stood my ground as a bachelor for a good many years—39 to be exact—some people believe that I am stubborn and somewhat set in my ways. This is not the case. It's simply that, in some matters, there is a right way and a wrong. As for cast iron, there are no if's, and's, and but's about it: either a skillet sticks or it doesn't.

Of course, my mother did some good cooking on a cast-iron skillet even after we got an electric stove. Moreover, my father had seven sisters who all cooked great food. Strangely, however, I didn't learn how to take proper care of a frying pan from my kinfolks. To be sure, I had observed my mother and my aunts wiping out a frying pan without putting it into the harsh, brown-soap dishwater. But the reasoning didn't sink in until I went to Auburn University.

During my college days, I quickly learned something of the art of cooking in a skillet on a one-eyed hotplate. But I had trouble with food sticking, and none of the engineering students were of much help. I took a job as a co-op engineering student at the nuclear bomb plant at Oak Ridge, Tennessee. While there, I shared a room with a fellow named Windell Nix, from the foothills of the Smokies in East Tennessee. A student of nuclear physics, Nix told me that I was washing the frying pan too much.

"My grandmother," he said, adding proof to the theory,

"has got a 13-inch cast-iron skillet that hasn't been washed for over a hundred years."

I laughed.

"I'm serious," he said, puffing up a little. "All she does is wipe it out with a cloth or paper toweling. You see—" He paused to light his pipe.

"I suppose she's married to the guy who hasn't cleaned the cake out of his pipe for 20 years?" I said.

But I smoked a pipe myself, and I knew all about what a good cake could do to make the smoke cool and mellow. So, I took Nix's word for the molecular theory of pipe cake and cast-iron seasoning, and quickly became a believer in keeping washing powders and scrub pads out of my frying pan.

Immediately the results became self-evident, and I've been eating good ever since.

In any case, once your cast-iron cookware takes a good seasoning, you simply must care for it. Scrubbing it with detergents and scouring pads will surely take out the seasoning. It can be rinsed in hot running water and wiped out immediately in case your dog has licked it or you have some other reason to suspect that it has germs in it. If, heaven forbid, it has chicken eggs or other food caked in it, try putting hot water in it and simmering it on a stove eye for a while. Then wipe it with a paper towel and rinse it in hot water. Dry it out thoroughly and coat it very lightly with bacon drippings. If you are lucky, it will be fine. If not, you'll have to start all over, as directed a little later.

As already indicated, putting a cast-iron piece in a dishwasher is very bad, partly because of the harsh detergent, the water jet, and the drying process. The worst thing you can do, however, is to leave it inside the machine (after the washing and rinsing cycles) in a very humid, hot environment.

After frying with cast iron, I merely pour off the grease and wipe the pan clean with a rag or paper towel. Then I store it in a dry place. Some kinds of cooking, as when baking cornbread, require that the surface of the cast iron be well greased. These pans are treated just like pans used for frying. Some other methods of cooking, as when making a stew in a Dutch oven, will not leave a well-defined coat of oil on the surface. Lightly I scrape the food out of these with a wooden spoon or rubber scraper, then I may rinse it under hot running water while wiping it clean with a sponge. Immediately I dry the pot and sit it on the stove eye, or in the oven, at very low heat for a few minutes. This warm environment will help dry the surface. Next, I put a very light coat of bacon drippings or cooking oil on the piece, inside and out, before putting it away.

In storage, by the way, it's best to give each piece its place and not stack it under or over something else. Never store a piece with a lid on it.

HOW TO SWEETEN THE POT

If foodstuff sticks to a cast-iron piece, be assured that it has been mistreated in one way or another, or else it was not properly seasoned to begin with. Fortunately, such a piece can be scoured out and re-seasoned. First, the pan is washed out thoroughly with (in this single instance) soap and water, then coated with grease and heated for a long period of time in the oven. All the manufacturer's information that I have seen, as well as suggestions in almost all cookbooks, say to coat the iron all over with a light coat of vegetable oil. I tried this several times—and ended up with a sticky surface that covered only part of the bottom of the pan. In one book, I noted that a specific brand of oil was specified. I bought some. But it didn't work either, not for me. I finally quit trying to follow the experts' directions and switched to ordinary bacon drippings. After all, I reasoned, our forefathers didn't normally have vegetable oil at hand. They had beef suet, lard, goose grease, or bear fat.

While writing this short work, by the way, I discovered that Lillian Bertram Marshall, in her *Southern Living Illustrated Cookbook,* had reached the same conclusion regarding vegetable oil. She pointed out that a bacon rind or hog skin was a good way to grease a cast-iron piece—a practice that was also used in the *Foxfire* books. But, alas, these days not many of us have a piece of hog skin handy when we need it. So, if you have neither skin nor bacon drippings, try wiping the pan inside and out with a piece (or half a strip) of bacon. Smoked bacon is great, but I would not recommend using salt pork or salt pork rind on cast iron.

In any case, after cleaning the piece and coating it with animal fat, put it into an oven at about 300 degrees for several hours. Cool the piece, wipe it out with a paper towel or rag, coat it again with animal fat, and bake it again at 300 degrees for several hours. After the first seasoning or two, the pan can be used for frying fish or chicken, provided that three-quarters of an inch of oil is used in the pan. Cooking in rather deep oil several times will in fact further the sweetening. It's best not to use the piece to fry eggs, to make country steak, or to simmer a thick stew until the cast iron has been seasoned *several* times.

There is no hard and fast rule to follow about the baking

times and temperatures required to achieve a proper seasoning, and in fact baking isn't always necessary. A pan can
also be seasoned on top of the stove, or in a campfire. Usually, however, the oven is the best way to go and the easi-
est.

Remember that new cast-iron pieces are coated with a
thin film of wax before they are shipped from the factory.
The wax helps prevent rust and keeps the piece looking
new. For cooking purposes, however, the wax must be removed and the piece must be seasoned, as directed above.
Once a piece takes a seasoning, it will cook good indefi-
nitely, and in fact it will get better with age, provided that it
is properly used. In time, a black cake may appear on the
sides of the pan, but this doesn't hurt a thing, in my opinion. In the book mentioned above, Lillian Marshall says that
if a heavily caked piece of cast iron is run through a regular
cycle in a self-cleaning oven, it will come out looking like
new. Damned if it doesn't!

Getting a piece of cast iron very hot either by accident or
for blackening a steak or a fish fillet may take out the seasoning. Usually, these pieces will take a new seasoning
readily, but of course the best practice is to keep your blackening griddle separate from the other pieces. Use it only for
blackening, and, after it has cooled, coat it *very* lightly with
oil.

I must add that sticking isn't the only problem with cast-
iron cookware that isn't seasoned properly. An ill-seasoned
piece can impart a metallic taste to food. Of course, this
usually occurs when meat is stewed for a long time in
tightly covered pieces, such as a Dutch oven with a good
lid. And, more often than not, the trouble will be in the
cast-iron lid. In any case, be sure to season the lid and the
sides of a cast-iron piece.

One major manufacturer of cast-iron cookware says that

iron getting into the food can be good for your health. Maybe. But I for one don't want enough of it to alter the taste of my food. How much iron will leave a properly seasoned cast-iron piece is questionable, at least to me. Frankly, I never see pits in my skillet or Dutch oven—a claim that I can't make for aluminum cookware.

Acidic foods tend to remove the seasoning from cast iron, resulting in a bad taste and discolored food. Never marinate meat in cast iron, especially if the marinade contains vinegar, buttermilk, or lots of salt.

Rust can be a problem with cast iron, but it usually results from improper storage together with inadequate seasoning. And from dishwashers.

Cast-Iron Skillet Specialties

Black iron is one of the oldest types of cookware in existence today. Columbus brought some with him to the New World in 1492. . . . Before that, during the reign of Edward III, from 1327 to 1377, iron pots and skillets were considered part of the "Crown Jewels."
—Diane Becker Finlay

A skillet is merely a cast-iron frying pan. Usually, but not always, a skillet has pouring spouts, or indented lips, set 90 degrees on either side of the handle. It was designed to hold enough oil or fat for frying, and of course frying is its main function. But remember, a cast-iron skillet, with a built-in handle, can also be used in the oven without danger of burning a plastic or wooden handle.

Skillets come in various sizes, from 5 inches in diameter up to 15 inches. A 15-inch skillet weighs over 9 pounds, and anything much larger would be too heavy for easy handling. A 20-inch skillet-like piece has recently been put on the market, but it doesn't have a regular handle; instead it has lifting nubs on either side. I don't think this is a true skillet, and it is discussed later. At the other extreme, a 5-inch skillet comes in handy for frying a chicken egg for breakfast, but it isn't much good for cooking bacon. There are some other tiny skillets on the market, but these were intended to be used as ashtrays or spoon holders. If I had to

A rectangular skillet comes in handy for cooking bacon.

choose one size skillet, it would surely be 10¼ inches wide. This is an ideal size for cooking on most stove eyes. But larger skillets will be needed for cooking some specialties, such as jambalaya.

Normally, skillets are round. But a square model is available. I like the square shape for cooking on coals or on a campfire, and I sometimes balance a square skillet on two bricks in my kitchen fireplace. A square skillet, however, on a round stove eye doesn't set too well with me aesthetically, although it is surely the best design for cooking bacon.

In any case, if you've got a well-sweetened cast-iron skillet of reasonable size, you can cook up some purely excellent victuals on the stovetop, by a campfire, or at the hearth. In short, a well-sweetened cast-iron skillet will cook anything that can be cooked in aluminum, stainless steel, or various Teflon-coated wares. Usually cast iron will cook better, too. Here are some recipes to try.

Country Steak

I allow that broiled T-bone steaks or grilled New York strips are hard to beat for dinner or supper, along with baked potatoes and salad. For breakfast, however, I'll take country steak and gravy every time. I normally use round steak for this dish, but about 15 minutes before this writing, my wife cooked up a batch of top sirloin to feed our strapling sons and a spend-the-night hulk or two. The flavor and texture were just right. For cooking this kind of steak for four people, I recommend a 12-inch cast-iron skillet. A griddle can be used for the steak itself, but doesn't work if you want lots of gravy, which ought to be a requirement for anything called country steak. Here's a recipe that has been used in my family for generations, and it is almost exactly like one used by my good wife's people.

beefsteak, ¾-inch thick	salt
cooking oil	pepper
flour	

Trim the steak and pound it with a meat mallet, edge of a heavy plate, or the mouth of a heavy glass bottle. (I use the edge of a plate, pounding in a criss-cross pattern; my wife uses an old, heavy 2-quart bottle, which she holds with both hands.) After you've worked over the meat, pour some flour in a plate and flip flop the steak in it. Then pound the steak again and flour it again. (Keep the flour plate handy.) Cut the steak into 3-inch pieces. Heat a little oil in a heavy skillet and cook the steak pieces on both sides until well browned. Remove the steak pieces to a heated serving platter. Pour off most of the grease. Draw a cup of water and have it ready. Using a tablespoon, put some flour into the skillet and stir it into the remaining grease and pan dredgings. Stir continuously on medium high heat until the mixture is browned, as when making a roux. Add water and stir until you have gravy of a consistency that suits your fancy. Salt and pepper to taste. The gravy can be served over the meat, or it can be served over rice or biscuit halves. For breakfast, I prefer biscuit halves. I don't require biscuits made from scratch if I've got a really good mix at hand. But I don't much care for the refrigerated canned biscuits.

Variation: The above recipe is what we usually make for breakfast. If we cook country steak for another meal, I usually add some onions to the gravy. Peel and dice a medium onion. Brown the onion for a couple of minutes in the skillet before adding the flour. Then proceed as usual. I am especially fond of this onion gravy, made quite thick and a little heavy on black pepper, served over fluffy white rice.

Smother-Fried Steak

My father had a way with very tough meat, and he was sometimes called upon to deal with difficult steaks. If you want to try his way, proceed with the recipe as described above. After the meat has been browned, put it aside. Thin the gravy with water and bring to a slow bubble. Then put the fried pieces of steak into the gravy, cover, reduce heat to very low, and simmer for 30 or 40 minutes, or until the meat is tender. (Check on the steak from time to time, making sure that it has enough moisture, and turn it over to prevent burning or sticking.) Serve the steak pieces with gravy direct from the skillet.

Venison Steaks

Many people take a hind leg of venison to a butcher and get it cut into "round steaks," but most home kitchens simply don't have the special equipment that is almost necessary to cut large pieces to a uniform thickness. If you butcher your venison at home, it's best to separate the leg muscles into smaller chunks. The chunks can be used for roasts, or, for this recipe, can be sliced into small steaks or chops. (The meat is easier to slice when it is cold.) I often cook venison by the recipe and technique above, but I normally beat it a little more than tough beef. When using my plate method, it's best to beat the meat one way and then beat it in a criss-cross pattern. Usually, we will use the smother-fry variation with venison, especially if it shows signs of being very tough.

Hamburger Steaks for Two

I once knew a cowpoke from Okeechobee City, Florida, who wouldn't eat beef unless it was ground up. He had good teeth and, so far as I could tell, he was perfectly able to chew. I decided that maybe he had never eaten a really good steak. What his wife cooked, I told myself, was hard and dry. I was wrong, of course, and, after eating her ground steak, I at least understood the man's position. Here's pretty much what the good woman did to make a believer out of me:

1 pound lean beef, ground	coarse black pepper
grease	hot black coffee
diced onion	whole wheat flour
salt	

Mix salt and pepper into the ground beef. Shape the meat into an oval pattie about 7 inches long. Heat a little grease in a cast-iron skillet. Brown the ground beef steak on one side for 5 or 6 minutes. Turn carefully. While the other side is browning, put a little whole wheat flour into the frying pan on one side of the oval steak. (There should be enough fat or pan liquid to moisten the flour; if not, add a tad of butter.) Stir the flour with a spoon and clear a spot for the onions. Stir the onions while they brown. If you've timed it right, the steak should be almost ready about now. Pour a little hot coffee atop the flour, and quickly stir in the onions. Let it bubble a few minutes, then spoon the gravy over the steak. Turn the steak over and halve it with your spatula. Check for doneness. I like mine medium rare, with a touch of pink showing in the center of the meat, provided that I've got freshly ground lean beef instead of old packaged (and repackaged) "hamburger meat." If you want yours well done, turn the heat to high and pour in a little more coffee. Quickly cover the skillet with a lid, thereby holding in the steam, and cook for a few minutes. When steamed this way, the steak can be well done without being too dry. But it's best if you don't overcook the meat. Serve the gravy over the steak. Feeds 2.

Herter's Minnesota Steak

In my book *Good Vittles*, I set forth a French skillet specialty called *steak au poivre*, and I can't repeat it here. Since then, I've experimented with a similar skillet steak as cooked by George Leonard Herter, co-author of *Bull Cook and Authentic Historical Recipes and Practices*. Herter was a great champion of beef suet, which he claimed was the only sensible substance to use for frying fish. Beef suet is difficult to find these days, and most grocery store employees don't even know the meaning of the term. It is, for the record, a beef shortening rendered from fat, especially from the good fat around the kidneys and other choice spots. Here's the complete list of ingredients for Herter's version:

steaks	**salt**
beef suet	**pepper**
butter, melted	

Put ⅛-inch of beef suet into a skillet. Salt and pepper the steaks to taste. Bring the skillet to heat and sear each side of the steak, then fry for three minutes or so on each side. Blot each side of the steak with a paper towel, then put the steak on a heated platter. Butter each side of the steak and serve hot.

I usually cook Herter's recipe after finding some T-bone steaks that weren't well trimmed and have lots of fat skirting the meat. I trim the fat closely, cut into ½-inch cubes, and fry enough of it, on low heat, in my cast-iron skillet until I have ⅛-inch of "suet." (Note that one T-bone steak will not always provide enough suet in which to cook itself, and more beef fat may be needed.) When you are finished rendering the suet, you'll have some small crackling-like balls left in the pan. Drain these on a brown paper bag and set them aside. Sear and fry the steak by the directions above, or, if you prefer, cook the steak on rather high heat and omit the searing step. Crumble the leftover beef cracklings and sprinkle them over a tossed salad, or use them to top the sour cream on your baked potato.

Note: People with cholesterol problems should beware of this recipe. The beef suet as well as the butter will up the count considerably.

Dan Webster's Stir-Fried Shrimp

"If you've got a good cast-iron skillet, you don't need a damned wok to stir-fry shrimp," Dan said, shaking a long wooden spoon at me as he spoke. "And you don't need soy stuff and monosodium glutamate, either."

Well, I quit arguing when I tasted the proof of the recipe:

fresh shrimp	lemons
butter	garlic

Juice the lemons, peel and crush the garlic, and melt the butter in a skillet. Mix lemon juice and garlic into the warm butter and put it aside while you peel the shrimp. When you are ready to cook, bring the butter mixture in the skillet to a medium high heat. Add the shrimp and stir them with a wooden spoon for 3 or 4 minutes; 5 or 6 minutes may be required for jumbo size. If you've got more than a pound of shrimp, cook them in separate batches. Do not overcook. Serve while hot. No sauce is required, but I like to use the pan drippings.

I asked Dan how much butter, garlic, and lemon juice he used per pound of shrimp. "Use as much as you need," he said.

Note: Stir-fry fans will be delighted to know that a cast-iron wok is now being manufactured in this country. See page 120.

Florida Hash

One of my favorite recipes, Florida hash, is best made with a large frying pan (about 14 inches wide). With smaller pans, cook the measures below in two batches.

2 cups fish flakes, pre-
  cooked
4 cups diced potatoes, pre-
  cooked
1 cup chopped onion
4 slices bacon

1 teaspoon salt
½ teaspoon pepper
½ tablespoon vinegar

If you are using fresh fish, boil or steam it for a few minutes, until it flakes easily. (Leftover fish can also be used.) Flake 2 cups and set aside. Dice 4 cups of peeled potatoes, boil until tender, drain, and set aside. Dice 4 slices of bacon. In a large frying pan, cook the bacon until it is almost done. Add the chopped onion and cook until the onion and bacon start to brown. While bacon and onion cook, mix fish, potatoes, salt, and pepper. Turn this mixture into the frying pan and spread evenly. On medium heat, cook until the bottom of the hash browns. Carefully turn the hash over and brown the other side. Sprinkle lightly with vinegar and serve. This dish goes nicely, with a large salad or lots of sliced tomatoes, for lunch or a light dinner. It also makes a hearty breakfast. Serves 4 to 6.

Skillet Barbecue

One of the best barbecue dishes that I've ever eaten is cooked in a large cast-iron skillet 12- or 13-inch) or in a stovetop Dutch oven. I've served it to guests on several occasions, with gratifying results. It goes best on a freezing night, when it's too cold to barbecue on the patio.

2 pounds lean beef, cubed
1 pound lean fresh pork,
  cubed
8 slices smoke-cured bacon

1 large onion, diced
1 large tomato, peeled and
  diced
3 cloves garlic, minced

1 cup catsup
½ cup vinegar
½ cup red wine
½ cup Worcestershire sauce

¼ cup dark brown sugar
½ tablespoon salt
½ teaspoon pepper
rice (cooked separately)

Fry the bacon in a large skillet (or Dutch oven) until it is crisp. Remove bacon and drain it on a brown paper bag. After trimming the pork and beef, cut it into cubes of about ¾-inch square. On medium high heat, brown the meat in the bacon drippings. Remove the meat from the skillet and drain it on the brown paper bag. Reduce heat to skillet and sauté the onions and garlic for 5 minutes. Add the diced tomato, red wine, vinegar, catsup, Worcestershire sauce, brown sugar, salt, and pepper. Add beef and pork to the skillet, along with crumbled bacon. Cover tightly. Simmer on low heat for an hour or so, stirring once or twice. Serve over rice. Feeds 6 or 7.

The popularity of "blackened redfish" a few years ago—almost a craze in some quarters—owed more to a radical cooking technique than to the fish itself. In fact, the redfish is nothing but an ordinary red drum. It's also called a channel bass, and small ones, less than 10 pounds, are sometimes called puppy drum.

Apparently, the original recipe for blackened redfish was created by professional chef Paul Prudhomme in Louisiana. My guess is that the dish was born of necessity when a cook accidentally burned somebody's order of pan fried fish, which happened to be the last fillet in Prudhomme's place! In any case, the popularity of the dish put an inordinate demand on the Gulf Coast commercial and sport fishery, in that it required redfish of a certain size. In order to blacken properly, a fish fillet has to be from ½- to ¾-inch thick. Ideally, fillets of this size must be taken from a relatively small redfish. This requirement for thin fillets, in turn, created a demand for these smaller fish, and helped spread the notion that larger redfish are not fit to eat. While it is true that large redfish (and they grow up to 80 pounds) are coarse and taste none too good, smaller fish, 15 pounds and under, are quite toothsome when cut into fingers and fried. (As always, the fish should be properly dressed and should be eaten fresh.) Many other kinds of fish are quite suitable for making "blackened redfish," including largemouth bass and walleyes. Even some rough fish can be blackened. A recent issue of *Outdoor Life* magazine, for example, set forth an article about a Texas couple who bagged alligator gar by bowfishing—and blackened the fillets.

Although much emphasis has been put on prepared Cajun "blackening" spice mixes, I think the real secret is of technique and specification. First, the cookware must be extremely hot, and cast iron is the only common cookware material that will withstand such temperatures. Second, the thickness of the fillet must be such that it will brown and form a crust on the outside while staying moist and succulent on the inside. Third, spices provide both flavor and crust, almost like a batter provides a crust in frying.

Be warned that true blackening produces clouds of smoke, and this rules out the kitchen stove. Even a stove with a powerful overhead vent may cause problems. Although I have blackened fish and meat successfully in a kitchen fireplace, I believe that it's best to take your blackening outside. But it is difficult to heat cast iron hot enough for true blackening, and remember that ordinary charcoal on a grill simply will not get hot enough to do the job. (Wood chips will help.) By far the best bet for obtaining the required heat is from a gas fired burner, such as those used for heating large fish fryers. Just any gas burner won't do. Some camp stoves, for example, won't put out enough heat. Also, a good deal depends on your cast-iron piece. In any case, cast-iron pieces will start turning white on the cooking surface when they are hot enough. Don't worry. It's hard to get cast iron too hot with normal cooking equipment.

Prudhomme used a large cast-iron skillet to illustrate the how-to pictures in one of his books. Another New Orleans sharp, Frank Davis, recommends (in *The Frank Davis Seafood Notebook*) that a cast-iron Dutch oven be used. I don't rec-

An oval cast-iron griddle is ideal for cooking
blackened redfish and similar dishes.

ommend either a skillet or a Dutch oven simply because the sides of these pieces are not needed for blackening and serve only as heat sinks. A cast-iron griddle is what you need, I say, and special "blackening" griddles of oval shape are now available. These are ideal.

Blackened Redfish

Having said that technique and exactness are the keys to this recipe, I'll have to add that the spice mix can be varied quite a bit. I prefer to use the spices set forth by *Chef Paul Prudhomme's Louisiana Kitchen*, although I change the proportions from one batch to the next. Hotness aside, I feel that lots of paprika is needed to give the spice mix body. It is very important that a thick coat of spices cover the fish flesh, and I use lots of paprika as a sort of filler. (I also cut back on the cayenne.) I've also seen other mixes. Frank Davis, for example, adds 12 crushed bay leaves and some basil, although he calls the recipe "Paul Prudhomme's Blackened Redfish." Also, *The Official Louisiana Seafood & Wild Game Cookbook* has fresh chopped parsley listed. (This work also specified fillets that are 1-inch thick, and said that a tablespoon of butter can be added to the hot skillet just ahead of the fish to prevent sticking. Be warned that a tablespoon of butter will smoke something awful and burn almost immediately. Also, I've never had a problem with any blackened food sticking, *if* the cast iron was hot enough.) In most recipes, the trend is to add stuff to the original, and the ingredients list for blackened redfish, already quite long, will continue to grow. It wouldn't surprise me to see monosodium glutamate listed.

In any case, here is my recommendation for blackened fish:

fish fillets (½- to ¾-inch thick)
melted butter
1 tablespoon salt
1 tablespoon Hungarian sweet paprika
½ teaspoon red cayenne, ground
1 teaspoon white pepper
1 teaspoon black pepper
1 teaspoon garlic powder
1 teaspoon onion powder
½ teaspoon crushed dried thyme leaves
½ teaspoon crushed dried oregano leaves

Mix the salt, spices, and herbs. Bring the fillets to room temperature. Melt the butter in a pan and coat each fillet on both sides. Sprinkle each fillet liberally with the spice mixture. Heat a griddle or skillet as hot as you can get it and warm some individual serving platters. Prepare bread, salad, cold drinks, etc., for serving. Get ready. Using tongs, hold a fillet by one end and lay it out on the super hot griddle. Sizzle for 2 minutes. Using tongs, flip the fillet over and sizzle the other side for 2 minutes. (Fillets that are only ½-inch thick will require even less cooking, and fillets that are 1 inch thick will require longer cooking.) Pick the fillet up with tongs and place it on a heated serving platter. Serve with melted butter as a sauce.

Alternate method: After turning the fillet, carefully spoon some melted butter onto the cooked side. Flop the fillet over when placing it on the serving platter, then spoon some butter onto the other side.

Blackened Beef

Following the popularity of blackened redfish, creative chefs and backyard jacklegs started blackening and burning other meats across the land, alarming local fire departments and polluting the atmosphere with smoke. My favorite spin-off recipe is for blackened beef, and I adapted it from an article in a special 80's issue of *Life* magazine. The success of the recipe depends in large part, I think, on the seasoned gravy. To make the dish, I use a skillet for the gravy and a griddle for the blackened beef.

SEASONINGS:

1 tablespoon salt	2½ teaspoons dry mustard
1 tablespoon and ¾-teaspoon black pepper	5 teaspoons fennel seeds
2½ teaspoons cayenne pepper	

Crush the fennel seeds and mix all ingredients. This seasoning will be used in both the gravy and on the meat. I prepare the gravy first so that it will be ready when the meat is blackened.

GRAVY:

1½ teaspoon blackening
  seasonings (from above)
⅓ cup cooking oil
⅔ cup flour

1 cup chopped green onion
  tops
4 cups beef or chicken stock

Heat the beef or chicken stock in a sauce pan and keep it warm. (You can also use plain water or water with bouillon cubes. Also, I have used a diluted ham stock with great success.) In a large skillet, heat the cooking oil and gradually stir in the flour. Cook very slowly for about 5 minutes, stirring constantly, until you have a medium brown roux. Remove the skillet from the heat and stir in the chopped green onion tops. Gradually stir in the warm stock and the seasonings. Put the skillet back on the heat, turn to high, and bring to a boil. Stir, reduce heat, and simmer uncovered for 15 minutes. Stir once or twice. During these 15 minutes, get your meat ready to cook so that both meat and gravy will be hot in temperature as well as in seasoning.

THE MEAT:

choice beef, preferably
  tenderloin, ¾-inch thick
melted butter

seasonings (from above)

Let the meat come to room temperature. Then dip each piece into melted butter. Sprinkle both sides of the meat generously with seasonings, and press some seasonings into the meat with your hands. Before cooking the meat, it's best to warm individual serving platters in an oven.

Heat an *ungreased* griddle (preferably oval) on very hot

wood coals or on a gas burner, as directed above. When the griddle is very hot, put one or two pieces of seasoned meat on it. Sizzle for 2 or 3 minutes, or until a crust forms on the bottom. Turn the meat with tongs and sizzle the other side for 2 or 3 minutes. Using tongs, place the meat onto the serving platter. Spoon on some hot gravy and serve with lots of good bread, green salad, baked potato—and lots of ice water.

Blackened Hamburger

Here's a spin-off dish that really doesn't belong in this section, so I'll keep it short. First, let me say that most ground beef contains too much fat to be properly blackened. The grease from the meat causes too much smoke and too much smell of burnt grease. (If you insist on real blackened hamburger, buy some very lean beef, trim it carefully, and grind it yourself.) With most of the commercially available ground meat, it's best to form patties about ¾-inch thick, add some salt and pepper to the meat, and broil it in an oven, so that the heat from the top causes the grease to drip out the bottom. If the meat is placed about 2 inches from the heat source, it can be cooked medium rare on the inside and well browned on the outside in about 3 minutes to each side. Then, serve on a heated platter with plenty of spicy gravy. Make up your own gravy mixture, or use the one set forth above. With hamburger, I really prefer lots of chopped onions as well as onion tops in my gravy.

Blackened Chicken

The regular blackening technique for fish and beef can also be used for chicken. Of course, the meat must be somewhat flattened and must not be too thick. Obviously, a blackened drumstick would be raw down next to the bone. By far the best bet is to use boned chicken breasts; then, with the smooth side of a wooden meat mallet, beat them down between two pieces of wax paper. For blackening, I like mine ½-inch thick.

A good spice mix for blackened chicken is available at supermarkets, and I usually use it instead of mixing my own. I do, however, sometimes blacken chicken with relatively tame spices, served for those who don't care for too much hot stuff. The trick here is to use lots of bright red Hungarian paprika. The secret of "blackened" meat depends, in part, upon having a crust of spices on both sides of the meat. Paprika can provide such a crust with only a small amount of hot pepper. However, I don't recommend that you start dumping the spice rack into a "blackened chicken" recipe, simply because some herbs don't work too well at such high temperatures. For openers, it's best to go with commercial blends or stick pretty much to hot pepper (black or white) and paprika, and maybe some powdered mustard. Red cayenne can also be used, but remember that it is very, very hot.

Blackened Duck and Geese

Breast of domestic duck can be blackened quite successfully. It's best to skin the duck, fillet out both sides of the breast, trim off any fat, and cook in exactly the same way as set forth above for beef. I use the same spice mix, and often cook the duck and beef together, giving my guests a choice of meats. Usually, a fillet of duck breast will be the right thickness to yield a crusty surface with a medium rare middle, which is ideal for both beef and duck, in my opinion.

Wild duck can be used successfully, but the breast fillets may not be quite thick enough for ideal blackening. Moreover, the meat of some wild ducks can be a bit strong for some tastes, in which case a 24-hour marinade of 1 tablespoon baking soda to 1 quart of water will help.

Breast fillets of wild and domestic geese can also be blackened. Fillets from large geese, however, may require flattening slightly with a wooden mallet. In fact, I've eaten some geese that could stand a bit of tenderizing with the toothed side of a meat mallet.

Other Griddle Specialties

A flat griddle, without high sides, cooks up a breakfast of sausage and scrambled chicken eggs in short order. Somehow, a spatula for turning eggs or pancakes just seems to work better on a griddle than on a skillet. Although most griddles are round, there are some square models on the market that are purely excellent for cooking bacon. The smaller griddles have a handle like a skillet, but some of the larger ones, usually rectangular in shape, have tab-like handles on either end and must be lifted with both hands.

Cast iron, when properly seasoned, is the ideal material for making griddles, partly because of its no-stick properties and partly because of its even heating. Cooking on griddles is covered in several other sections of this book, and here I'll include only a couple of recipes that are especially suited for one-handed models of normal size.

Open-Faced Griddle Omelet

Omelets are usually cooked in a special pan, but I am fond of a cheese and fish flake omelet that is cooked on a flat, 12-inch pancake griddle both on top of the stove and under the broiler. I usually make it with leftover fish, either fried, baked, or broiled. Here's how:

4 chicken eggs	1 strip bacon
1 cup fish flakes (precooked)	grated cheese

Preheat the broiler and adjust the rack so that it is very close to the heating unit. Break the eggs into a bowl and whisk them lightly. Set aside. Heat the griddle on the stovetop and fry the strip of bacon until it is crisp. Crumble the bacon and set it aside. Pour off the excess bacon grease. Put the fish flakes onto the griddle and sauté them for two or three minutes. Add the eggs, stir with a spatula, and cook on low heat until the eggs are partly set. Remove the griddle from the heat. Sprinkle the eggs lightly with the cheese and put the griddle into the oven directly under the broiler. Broil until the cheese starts to brown. Remove the griddle and sprinkle the omelet with crumbled bacon. Serves 2.

Variations on this dish are infinite, and I'll sometimes sprinkle chopped tomatoes, chopped onions, etc., on top of the eggs, with or without cheese.

Whole Wheat Flapjacks

The cast-iron griddle is, of course, ideal for cooking pancakes or flapjacks (as I call them). In fact, pancakes are often called griddle cakes. A number of packaged pancake mixes are good, or you can try my whole wheat and buttermilk recipe.

1½ cups whole wheat flour
1 medium chicken egg
2½ teaspoons baking
  powder
1 cup buttermilk

2 tablespoons bacon
  drippings
1 tablespoon sugar
1 teaspoon salt

Mix the flour, baking powder, sugar, and salt in a bowl. In another bowl, whisk the egg and mix in the buttermilk and bacon drippings. Mix the contents of the two bowls, stirring until you have a smooth batter. Heat your griddle, but do not grease it. Drop the batter onto the griddle by the spoonful, allowing almost ¼ cup of batter for each pancake. Cook until bubbles appear on the top. Turn and cook on the other side. (Usually, the underside will be ready when the top side responds to the touch test. Stick your finger lightly into the pancake and then quickly draw it back. If the finger leaves a deep indentation, the pancake isn't ready. When done, the pancake will more or less spring back into shape.)

As it happened, I cooked the above recipe only half an hour before writing these few paragraphs. When I got up this morning, the weather was cold but the sun was out and there wasn't a cloud in the blue sky. A north wind blew. I had to take one of my children somewhere, and on the way I saw a man sitting in a wheelchair in the sun on the east side of his house, out of the wind. For some reason, he waved at me. Maybe he thought he knew me. Looking sickly, he was well bundled up in what looked like a plaid afghan. He smoked a cigar.

As I drove on, I started counting my blessings. On the way back, I stopped at a grocery store and bought a pound of real butter. At home, I started coffee brewing, mixed up a batch of flapjacks, and opened a small jar of thick, dark wild honey to pour over them. Flapjacks rank high on things that make life worth living.

(Also see Sourdough flapjacks, page 103.)

Sizzled Fish

Some fish fillets are difficult to turn on a grill or under a broiler. Crappie fillets, for example, easily tear apart, especially when they are skinned. Using an oval-shaped griddle with a rattan base, I developed a method of dealing with these easily flaked fillets. In short, I cook the fillet without turning it and then serve it on the same cast-iron piece. The trick is to preheat the broiler and adjust the rack so that it is very close to the heating elements. Then grease and heat the griddle on the eye of the stove. When the griddle is quite hot, put the fish fillet on it. Quickly brush on a little butter and garlic sauce, sprinkle with salt and white pepper, and put it immediately under the broiler. Within two or three minutes, remove the griddle from the broiler. (Remember that the hot griddle will cook the bottom of the fillet while the broiler cooks the top. Thick fillets will take longer to cook. If in doubt, test the fish with a fork. It is done when it flakes easily. Do not overcook.) Garnish the fillet with a slice of lemon and fresh parsley. Serve with hot bread, asparagus, or other cooked vegetables.

Dutch Oven Specialties

Ed was of the great amateur cooks of this world, and with the simplest Florida backwoods ingredients and a Dutch oven, turned out dishes so superlative that when I now prepare one, I grieve that Ed is not here to partake.
—Marjorie Kinnan Rawlings, *Cross Creek Cookery*

There are two kinds of Dutch oven. The one usually found in the modern kitchen has a dome-shaped lid and is flat on the bottom. It is, of course, ideal for cooking on top of a stove, and it is discussed a little later. The other kind, sometimes called a camp oven, is ideal for cooking everything from bread to stew meat over a campfire or at a home fireplace hearth.

The camp Dutch oven became the most important piece

The popular Dutch oven can be used as a stove top pot or it can be suspended over a campfire. It's great for long, slow cooking.

of cookware in the westward expansion, simply because it was so versatile. It is still a highly desirable piece of gear for any remote camp, or on camping trips, where an oven and other modern gear is not available. In it, a camper can cook everything he needs—even bread. At home, a camp oven can come in handy, during electric power failures, for cooking on the family hearth or in the yard. Fortunately for the sportsman, the Dutch oven is manufactured today pretty much like it was in the 1800's.

Unlike the stovetop version, the camp oven has legs so that it sits over coals. It also has a flanged lid, which is recessed so that it can hold coals on top. This feature comes in very, very handy for baking bread, for cooking stews for a long time, and for keeping foods warm. The flat lid can also serve as a griddle or a shallow skillet.

The inventor of the original Dutch oven remains in question, and some writers speculate that Paul Revere designed it. In all probability, the more or less final shape of this versatile piece of cookware came about in steps, evolving to suit the needs of the American settler and the westward expansion. Most modern authorities believe the term "Dutch" to have come about because the cookware was

The old camp Dutch oven was an important piece of gear during frontier days. Hot coals were piled onto the lid in order to brown the biscuits. This original Dutch oven is still being manufactured today for camp or fireplace cookery.

sold by Dutch peddlers. But I wonder. The so-called Pennsylvania Dutch settlers also came up with a large oven, made with stone and mortar. These were usually built in connection with a spring house or a smokehouse, and were not a part of the hearth. A large fire was built inside the oven. When a high temperature was attained, the fire was extinguished and the baking started. The good women of these Pennsylvania settlements gained fame in baking pies, and, who knows, the term "Dutch oven" might have started here. If so, it should be called the "Deutsch oven."

The real Dutch settlers, who established a trading post on Manhattan Island in 1614, also developed a Dutch oven, which was built into the end of the fireplace. They also used cast-iron pieces for baking. Here's an account from Gertrude I. Thomas's *Foods of our Forefathers*: "Plenty of baking was carried on in a Dutch oven which was an improvement over the roasting kitchen of Virginia. It was cylindrical and open to the fire on one side, and through it ran a spit for roasting the meat. Bread and cakes were baked in heavy iron kettles with convex, curved lids, into which were piled the live coals."

Whatever the truth about the name "Dutch oven," a number of more fanciful explanations have been set forth, sometimes in jest. In a 1971 edition of *Field & Stream*, for example, Ted Trueblood attributed the name to one Dutch O'Leary, a "celebrated frontiersman." And a trapper named Steeljaws Newhouse (Trueblood went on) added the lid with an upturned rim for holding coals on top of the oven. But I suspect that Ted Trueblood had a lot of fun with names, including his own.

In any case, the Dutch oven was an important piece of gear to some of the frontier people. If you do much camp fire cooking, or like to cook in your fireplace at home, as I do, I strongly urge you to purchase a Dutch oven of this type. Here are a few recipes:

Camp Biscuits

Making good biscuits in a camp Dutch oven is easy, provided that you preheat the oven properly. Most any biscuit recipe that can be cooked at home can be cooked over coals. For starters, I recommend that you buy a good biscuit mix and follow the directions on the package. For convenience, the small boxes (7-ounce size) of biscuit mix work well and are easy to pack. Of course, if you have a favorite recipe, use it. In any case, the first step toward toothsome biscuits is to build a good fire. You'll need lots of coals, so put on lots of wood. A good hard wood, such as oak, is the best bet. Cured wood makes coals faster, but green or freshly cut wood can be used if necessary. Avoid rotten wood, if possible. Both green and rotten woods make more smoke, as moonshiners know.

Pull out a bed of coals and put the Dutch oven lid on them. Then put the pot on top of the lid. Mix the biscuit ingredients while the oven is preheating. Take the oven off the coals and grease it lightly. Tear off pieces of the biscuit dough and place them in the bottom of the Dutch oven, arranging them so that they touch but do not squeeze in. Put the pot on the bed of coals and cover it with the lid. Then pile fresh red-hot coals onto the lid.

In 15 minutes, remove the lid with a lid hook, being careful not to spill any ashes. If the biscuits are not browned, replace the lid for a few more minutes.

After you cook a couple of batches of ordinary biscuits, you might want to try the recipe in the Sourdough section (starting on page 97).

All-Day Pot Roast

The best way to cook roasts or other large chunks of meat in camp is to dig a hole, put plenty of hot coals in it, put the Dutch oven on top of the coals, and pile more coals on top of the lid. Then cover it all up with the dirt that came out of the hole. Remember, however, that digging a hole in the woods is often something of a problem, especially if roots or rocks, or both, are present. You'll need a scoop. Dig the hole deeper and wider than the Dutch oven, then build a large fire on top of the hole. Then build another fire nearby. (One fire will do, but remember that you will need two batches of coals: one for the bottom of the pit and one to go atop the Dutch oven lid.)

Some people pack along charcoal for cooking purposes, and of course it works nicely for pit cooking. But remember that you'll need lots of it, which can make camp cooking a little expensive. On the other hand, I must point out that Dutch oven specialists can define exactly how many briquets are required on top and bottom for cooking a certain recipe in a Dutch oven of a certain size. In any case, here's a good recipe to try:

beef or venison roast, about 6 pounds	carrots
cooking oil	onions
flour	salt and pepper
potatoes	

Dig the pit and build the fire early in the morning. When the fire has burned down somewhat, rake out some coals and heat a little oil in the bottom part of the Dutch oven. Sprinkle the roast with flour and brown it on all sides in the hot oil. (In other words, you need to brown the roast in the pot before putting it into the pit.) Salt and pepper the roast. Add two cups of water and put the lid on top. Peel the onions and potatoes, then scrape the carrots. Put the potatoes and carrots around the roast, then add the onions on top. Sprinkle on a little salt and pepper. The exact measures of the vegetables aren't too important, so feel free to fill up the pot if you have lots of folks to feed.

From the fire directly over the pit, rake all the coals into the hole. Lower the Dutch oven directly onto the coals. Pile coals from the second fire onto the lid. Then fill up the hole and pile dirt on top. Leave the pot in the hole for 7 to 10 hours, while you are out hunting or fishing or shooting pictures. Before leaving camp, however, make sure that the two fires are out. When you get back, you'll have a complete dinner ready. You'll have gravy, too. Feeds 8 to 12.

Note: The technique above can be used to cook a number of recipes for large chunks of meat, and it will also work with various recipes calling for stew meat. Remember also that such recipes don't need lots of water or liquid, if the lid fits tightly. (See "lids," starting on page 134.)

Camp Stew

Although a purely excellent stew can be cooked by the pit method described above, all-day cooking may not always be practical. A good stew can be made in an hour or two on good campfire coals. Having legs, the camp Dutch oven is ideal in that it sits over a bed of coals but not directly on them. (Direct contact with a flat pan will actually extinguish the coals.) Also remember that you can start cooking with a Dutch oven even before the fire has burned down and made coals. The Dutch oven has a bail attached to the pot, which permits it to be hung over the flames. I've always found a sturdy tripod with a drop chain and an S-hook is by far the best for this purpose, although some people are a-dept with a dingle stick. If you have a choice, however, wait for the coals. In any case, here's a stew recipe to try in camp.

2 pounds lean stew meat	2 medium potatoes
flour (optional)	2 carrots
cooking oil (optional)	salt and pepper
2 medium onions	water

I realize that the list of ingredients for this dish is almost the same as for the pot roast. The reason is that onions, potatoes, and carrots are easy to transport and store in camp, as compared to some other vegetables. Also, in the pot roast these same vegetables were used whole (for very long cooking) whereas in this recipe they are cut up.

If you have oil and are cooking on coals, dust the meat with flour and brown it. Then peel and quarter the potatoes and onions. Scrape and chop the carrots. Add the vegetables to the meat and pour in two cups of water. Salt and pepper to taste. Cover and cook for an hour or longer, stirring from time to time to prevent the bottom from burning. Add water if needed. Add more coals around the pot, if needed, and push some underneath. This recipe will feed 4 campers.

Note: If you have a grill fitted over your campfire, your camp Dutch oven can usually be used on it. The legs will probably fit into the holes or cracks.

If you plan to start cooking by hanging the Dutch oven over flames, load the pot with carrots, meat, potatoes, and onions, in that order, then add salt, pepper, and water. Cover tightly and suspend the pot over the fire. Omit the cooking oil and the flour. Cook until the meat is done and the potatoes are tender when tested with a fork. It's best to stir the contents from time to time, and add more water if needed. It's also best to swing the pot away from the fire before you remove the lid and stir the dish.

Big Scrub Guinea Hen

In *Cross Creek Cookery*, Mrs. Rawlings said that it was Ed Hopkins who introduced her to the people in Florida's Big Scrub area, where she set such works as *The Yearling*. Here's a recipe that, I feel, came from Hopkins or from the Scrub people. In any case, I include the recipe in this little book not only because it is good but also because it uses the heated Dutch oven lid to brown the top of a piece of meat while, at the same time, browning the bottom as usual. (I might add that some purely excellent cooks pride themselves in *browning* the bottom of a dish without actually burning it. In Iran, for example, certain rice dishes are browned on the bottom, and the crusty part, considered a delicacy, is saved for the elders.) Heavy cast-iron cookware is ideal for this skill. Don't try it in thin metal cookware coated with Teflon on a campfire, or anywhere else. Here's what you'll need:

FOR THE DUTCH OVEN:

1 guinea hen	carrots
water	medium-sized potatoes

FOR STUFFING AND PASTE:

bread	¼ cup flour
sage	¼ cup butter
chopped onion	½ teaspoon salt

Mix a stuffing of bread, sage, and chopped onion. Salt and pepper the inside of the guinea hen, then stuff it. (I also like to boil the guinea hen giblets until tender, chop them, and add them to the stuffing.) Place the stuffed guinea hen into the Dutch oven, breast side up. Add two cups hot water. Put the Dutch oven on hot coals and cover with the lid. Pile hot coals atop the lid. Cook for half an hour. Peel the potatoes and scrape the carrots with your knife, then add both to the pot. (When you remove the lid, check to see whether the guinea hen's breast has browned. If it has, do not replenish coals in the lid. If it hasn't browned, check it again after cooking another 20 minutes or so.) Cover again and cook for an hour. After that time, the potatoes and carrots should be tender. Remove the guinea hen and vegetables.

Ideally, the liquid will have cooked down very low and will have browned on the bottom. If it hasn't, continue cooking over the coals. Do not burn. If you want gravy, stir in 2 tablespoons of flour and ½ teaspoon salt. Stir well. Slowly add two cups of water, then continue to cook and stir until you have the gravy as thick as you want it. Serves 2 or 3.

Note: I have been faithful to the list of ingredients used in this dish, but I have elaborated somewhat on the cooking technique. Ed Hopkins might put all this stuff in a Dutch oven and open the lid at the exact time when the pan drippings have browned perfectly on the bottom, but I feel that most of us, without daily practice, will need to take a peek or two.

Variations: If you don't have a guinea hen at your place, or can't catch one, you might try a pullet or a pheasant. I recently used the technique to cook a domestic duck, skinned. It was super good, and I wished that Mrs. Rawlings and Ed Hopkins were there to partake of it.

Venison Liver and Onions on the Lid

Just because you've got a Dutch oven in camp doesn't mean that you have to use all of it, and build a large fire, in order to cook a good meal. Remember that the lid can be used over coals to pan fry fish, chops, and so on. One of my favorite camp meals makes use of fresh venison liver, and it can be prepared on a Dutch oven lid. It's easy, and doesn't require a long list of ingredients.

venison liver	**medium onion**
bacon	**salt and pepper**
flour	**water**

Trim the liver, wash it, and cut it into fingers about ½-inch thick. Salt and pepper the strips and shake them in flour. Leave them in the flour for the time being. Fry the bacon on the lid until browned. Take it up and set it aside to drain, preferably on a brown paper bag. Slice the onion, separate the slices into rings, and sauté them in the bacon drippings for five minutes. Take up the onions and put them aside to drain. Brown the strips of liver on both sides for a few minutes. Do not overcook the liver. (If your lid is hot, and produces a good sizzle, cooking the liver for 3 minutes on each side will be about right, if the pieces are ½-

inch thick.) When the liver is almost done, crumble the bacon and add it to the lid. Add the onions. Pour on a little water and cook for 5 minutes. Serve from the lid, spooning liver, onions, and pan drippings directly onto plates.

Variations: The last time I prepared this dish, I used diced salt pork instead of bacon. I also added a wild turkey liver to the venison liver, along with some fresh mushrooms. It was all very tasty. Rabbit liver is also very good when cooked by this recipe. And fresh chicken liver is almost as good.

Easy Camp Breakfast

The lid to the Dutch oven will do for frying up a little bacon and a chicken egg or two. If you don't have eggs (or have broken them, as often happens in camp), try my recipe for breakfast potatoes and bacon:

bacon, thick sliced	salt
potatoes, sliced ¼-inch thick, unpeeled	

Build a fire and brew some coffee. When you have enough hot coals, rake some aside and form a bed. Place the Dutch oven lid on the coals and put the bacon on it. Stand by while it cooks. If the bacon seems about to burn, pick up the lid with your hook and hold it up while it cools a bit. You may have to repeat this step a few times, but chances are that the heat will be at least in the ballpark. When the bacon is crisp, take it up and put it on a brown paper bag to drain. (If you don't have a brown bag or absorbent paper, put it on a plate or some suitable surface.) Fry the potatoes in the bacon drippings, turning from time to time so that they don't burn on the bottom. Take up the sliced potatoes and put them on the brown bag to drain. Salt the potatoes to taste.

I admit that this recipe isn't much for variety, but it's a hearty dish that will stick with you during a hard day afield. And it's easy. Remember also that eggs can be fried to go along with the potatoes and bacon, and toast can also be made in the Dutch oven lid.

Note: Sliced potatoes fried in bacon grease on a cast-iron griddle or frying pan is also a very tasty addition to a meal cooked at home. If you want to get fancy, separate the potatoes when you put them on paper for draining, then sprinkle the tops lightly with bright red paprika.

Camp Snacks

Your camp Dutch oven is ideal for cooking popcorn, which, of course, is very easy to transport and store. Merely heat the Dutch oven over coals and pour in some popcorn kernels. You might also consider parched corn, which is also easily cooked on a Dutch oven. Here's a quote from an article by Don Holm ("Dutch Oven Cookery") from the October 1972 issue of *Sports Afield:*

"How do you suppose the voyageurs paddled Hudson's Bay Company freight canoes all the way from Montreal to Fort Vancouver, packing most of their rations with them? They practically lived on parched corn.

"Preheat Dutch oven on hot coals. Do not use water or grease. Drop in shelled sweet corn kernels and toast them, turning or stirring frequently to keep from burning. When corn is brown and crunchy it is done.

"Like pemmican, parched corn is an ideal trail food, light

and easily stored for long periods. It was a staple of the French-Canadians, the fur traders, and mountain men, as well as Indian tribes like the Arikaras and Mandans."

Parched corn, by the way, can be eaten warm or cold. I prefer mine warm, with a touch of salt and a cold beer.

In 1813, when mountain man John Colter died of yellow jaundice, his Dutch oven sold for $4, the equivalent of a week's wages then. The iron pots were used not only for cooking but for boiling water to obtain salt at salt licks, melting lead for casting rifle balls, and as ransom to Indians.
—J. Wayne Fears, *Sports Afield*

STOVETOP DUTCH OVENS

Unlike the camp Dutch oven, the stovetop model has neither legs nor a flanged lid. It's flat on the bottom and has a domed lid on top. The lid is usually made of cast iron, but glass lids are also available. My personal choice is a heavy cast-iron lid with little equidistant protuberances underneath, so that condensation drips down evenly. Such a lid is called "self-basting."

This kind of Dutch oven was, of course, designed for sitting on top of a kitchen stove. Nevertheless, it can be used in camp and it can also be put into an oven. But it is primarily a stovetop piece, and as such it is hard to beat for cooking pot roasts, stews, fish chowders, and other dishes that gain from slow, even cooking in a tightly covered pot. The Dutch oven can also be used, to great advantage, as a deep fryer. Remember, however, that a large Dutch oven may not work on a small one-burner camp stove simply because it dissipates too much heat.

Thousands of good recipes could be listed below, and any good family cookbook will have directions for various stews and pot roasts. I am, however, adding two of my favorites, both of which happen to be Irish in origin. Personally, I don't make too much of the Irish connection, but I have a friend who says that the Dutch oven was really invented by the Irish—the folk who also, he claims, invented cast iron itself and discovered thyme.

Struisin Gaelach

My friend puffs up and turns red of face when I tell him that Irish potatoes, which is a name often given to ordinary Idaho potatoes, originally came from America. Whatever he says, it follows that Irish stew really ought to be called American stew, since it has a potato base, although, I allow, some people make it with turnip roots instead of potatoes. In any case, my recipe was adapted from *Traditional Irish Recipes* by George L. Thomson.

3 pounds lamb, cubed	½ tablespoon parsley
2 pounds potatoes	1 teaspoon thyme
1 pound tomatoes	1 teaspoon salt
1½ cups meat stock or bouillon	½ teaspoon pepper

If feasible, select both large and small potatoes and onions. Preheat the oven to 325 degrees. Slice a large potato and line the bottom of a Dutch oven with the slices. Peel the onions, slice one, and add a layer above the potatoes. Trim the meat and put it on top of the onions. On top of the meat, put the rest of the onions, either whole or quartered.

Sprinkle on the thyme, salt, and pepper. Next, add the rest of the potatoes, either whole or quartered, depending on size; peeled or unpeeled, depending on preference. Add the stock. Cover tightly and put into the preheated oven. Cook for 2 hours without peeking. Serves 6 to 8.

This same recipe also makes a great camp dish, partly because it doesn't require lots of dainty or fragile ingredients, such as chicken eggs. Of course, the recipe can be cooked in a camp Dutch oven.

Anraith Bhainbh

The Irish also have a dish called grunt soup, made with small perch. I tried it with American bluegills and some chopped onions (which were not in the original recipe). It was delicious, and I want to pass it on. Because the name "grunt soup" doesn't sound too good, I'm going back to the Gaelic for the name. If you want to try my version of *anraith bhainbh*, here's what you'll need:

12 bluegills or other small fish	½ tablespoon dried chopped parsley
1 quart water	½ tablespoon dried chopped chives
½ stick margarine	½ teaspoon salt
1 medium onion	¼ teaspoon pepper
1 tablespoon flour	

Scale the fish and clean them. I leave the heads on, but this is optional. Put the fish into a Dutch oven and pour in 1 quart of water. Add the salt. Bring to a boil, then reduce the heat and simmer for a few minutes, or until the fish flakes easily from the bone. While the fish are simmering, melt the margarine in a skillet and chop the onion. Sauté the onion for about 3 or 4 minutes, then stir in the flour slowly. Leave the skillet on very low heat. Meanwhile, remove the fish from the Dutch oven and drain in a colander. (Be careful not to leave any fins or parts of the fish in the liquid.) Turn the Dutch oven heat up just a little and gently boil the liquid, uncovered.

Using a fork, carefully pull the meat from the fish bones. And stir the flour from time to time. After about 10 minutes (or quicker if the onions are getting too brown), add the roux to the liquid in the Dutch oven. Also add the chives, parsley, and pepper. Finish pulling the meat from the fish bones. Add the fish to the Dutch oven and simmer for 10 minutes. Serve as an appetizer or as a meal, along with boiled potatoes, bread, green vegetable, and salad.

Camp Variation: This recipe can also be cooked with a camp Dutch oven. Merely use the lid of the Dutch oven instead of a skillet to brown the onions and roux. Also, try the recipe with wild onions instead of regular onions, using the fresh green tops instead of the parsley and chives.

Note: Any good fish of mild flavor can be used in the recipe above. I make it more often with bluegills simply because I, or my children, catch lots of them. I've also made it with crappie heads. Of course, fish heads contain some of the best meat, but most people throw them out. Whether you use heads or whole fish, make sure that you get all the bones out before putting the meat into the soup. Gnawing on fish heads is permitted only in the privacy of the kitchen, not at the dining table.

Dutch Oven Venison

The following recipe illustrates how a Dutch oven can be used on top of the stove or in the oven, or both, and how to first brown the meat and then to "braise" it. A meat rack is also used, and, I might add, an 8-inch cast-iron rack (also called a trivet) is manufactured especially for Dutch ovens. The recipe comes from *Alaska Magazine's Cabin Cookbook,* which explains, "Sometimes a deer has lived too long to yield tender steaks and roasts, and that is when we must resort to braising.

"Cut the venison into serving-size pieces and dredge with whole wheat flour. Season with salt, pepper, and any other seasonings you wish. Thyme and marjoram are both good here, as well as dried bell pepper pieces and minced onions. . . .

"Heat about ¼ inch of fat in a Dutch oven and brown the meat slowly in the fat, turning the pieces to ensure even browning. Then put a rack under the meat, add about ¼ cup of water, and cover the pan tightly. Continue cooking over low heat or in a slow oven (300 degrees) until tender (about 1½ to 2 hours). Add a little more water from time to time if necessary to keep the venison from scorching."

The above recipe makes very good gravy, and I am fond of using it to cook lean beef as well as venison.

Cast-Iron Pots and Pans

At one time, most of our domestic cooking was done by hanging a pot over a fire. In camp, a tripod, dingle stick, or some other mechanical device was used for suspending the pot over the flames or coals. In the home fireplace, some sort of built-in crossbar or crane was used to hold the pots. Of course, various kinds of hooks and chains were used at home and in camp for holding the pots at just the right height, while allowing them to be swung free of the flame for easy stirring. Almost all pots had bails, and some of them also had legs on the bottom.

Although the stovetop Dutch oven has pretty much taken over the role of the cast-iron pot and pan, a few models are still being made. Lodge Manufacturing Company, for example, makes a flat-bottom pot (which they call a kettle) for

Cast-iron kettles, once popular for fireplace cooking, make great pots for cooking atop a modern stove.

The campfire kettle is ideal for sitting over a bed of hot coals, or for suspending over the fire by the bail.

stovetop cooking; they also make a round bottom pot with legs and a bail, designed for camp cooking. Lids are available for both models. These pots, deeper than Dutch ovens, are said to be the traditional bean pot.

I don't offer many recipes for these kinds of pots and pans, partly because they are not commonly used today. But they have had a great influence on our traditional American cooking, and most of the recipes for meat pies (which we usually put into the oven) were developed in a pot. Some of the older pots had lids that held coals, so that the top of the food inside would be browned. This idea no doubt led to the Dutch oven. Note also that some of the

Some modern cast-iron pots, or saucepans, are convenient for stove top cooking. The cast-iron handle permits the piece to be put into the oven.

older potpies did not have a browned crust, going instead for a soft dumpling-like top. Further, the hearthside cooks of yesteryear made good use of a long iron rod called a salamander. One end of this tool was heated red hot in the coals, then held over the surface of food that needed browning.

A pot or kettle has a bail-type handle, suitable for hanging the piece over a fire or coals. A pan, however, has a handle. You don't see many cast-iron pans today, but they are still available and should be used more frequently, especially in view of the fact that the cast-in handle is ovenproof. Called either stew pans or sauce pans, these pieces usually come with a cast-iron lid. Some cast-iron pieces of similar shape come with a wire basket and are called French fryers.

Pots with bails are still quite useful for cooking over an open fire, but they are not as versatile as the Dutch oven. In any case, here's a great American recipe that was developed with the aid of a cast-iron pot:

Brunswick Stew

According to *The Art of American Indian Cooking*, the original Brunswick stew was made by the Powhatan, Chickahominy, and Cherokee tribes. It contained meat from small game and fowl, along with native vegetables, namely, corn, beans, and tomatoes. Potatoes, I might add, are also native American vegetables, and these days they are usually included in any list of Brunswick stew ingredients.

According to the Indian book, the term "Brunswick stew" came from the British settlers at Jamestown. The Indians, I am sure, cooked the stew in a clay pot, but the settlers brought cast-iron pots with them and no doubt cooked the stew over an open fire. Today, the dish can be made in a pot over the fire, in a pot on the stove, or in a Dutch oven type utensil. In any case, it requires long, slow cooking—especially if it is made with tough squirrels.

Typically, Brunswick stew is a rather bland dish, as compared to the chili made by the Indian tribes of the Southwest. My favorite is made with cottontail rabbit or the small marsh rabbits, but of course it can be made with a variety of meats, including even a tough barnyard rooster:

5 gray squirrels, 3 fox squirrels, 2 cottontails, or 2 tough pheasants
water
2 large onions, peeled and quartered
2 large potatoes, quartered
2 cups fresh or frozen whole kernel corn
2 cups fresh or baby lima beans (or butterbeans)

6 fresh tomatoes, peeled and quartered
1 stalk celery, chopped
1 tablespoon parsley
3 bay leaves
1 tablespoon salt
½ teaspoon pepper

When you field dress the game and fowl, be sure to save the liver, heart, gizzard, and neck. To cook, put all the meat and giblets into a cast-iron pot of suitable size. Add 3 bay leaves and cover the meat with water. Bring to a boil, reduce heat, and simmer for 2 hours, or until the meat is done. Discard the bay leaves. Put the meat aside to drain. Skim any surface scum off the liquid. Into the pot put the salt, pepper, celery, parsley, potatoes, beans, corn, and onions. Cover tightly and simmer on very low heat for 30 minutes. Peel the tomatoes, quarter them, and add to the pot. Bone the meat and add it to the vegetables. Simmer for another 20 minutes. Serve hot in soup bowls. Feeds 8 to 10.

Remember that there must be a thousand recipes for

Brunswick stew. One popular ingredient is a little "season-ing meat," such as ½ pound of salt pork. While this makes good eating, remember it also adds fat. For flavor, I like to cube a pound of salt pork and fry out the fat in a cast-iron skillet. I discard the grease and put the cubed meat into the stew.

In Camp: Use canned lima beans, corn, and tomatoes, but stick with fresh potatoes and onions, if possible. Omit the parsley, or maybe substitute a handful of fresh watercress or wild onion tops for the parsley.

Fried Chicken and Fish

Heavy black cast-iron pots, caldrons, and skillets are a leit-
motiv of Black cooking. Without them there is no Brazilian
Acaraje, no Nigeriar, Akkra Fun Fun, no Fried Fish Baxter's
Road style in Barbados, and no Southern Fried Chicken.
    —Jessica Harris, Iron Pots and Wooden Spoons

When doing TV commercials
a few years ago, a famous country music star said that
chicken fried in a certain brand of vegetable shortening
doesn't taste greasy. After seeing the commercial several
times, my young son told my wife not to buy any of the
shortening. Why? He *wanted* his fried chicken to be greasy.
He didn't necessarily mean to imply that the chicken should
be soggy or dripping oil, but the boy had a point. Fried
chicken simply isn't up to par if there is no imperative to
lick the fingers after finishing off a drumstick. Also, fried
chicken should have crunch, which is produced best by hot
oil and a batter.

Even so, the prudent cook can still cook up tasty chicken
while at the same time reducing the fat. Here's my recipe,
guaranteed to keep the kids at home, reduce the divorce
rate, bring the preachers to Sunday dinner, and preserve
the American way. You'll need only a few simple ingredients and a cast-iron skillet.

Family Chicken

The measures in this simple recipe depend on how many folks you've got to feed. Usually, a fryer of normal size will satisfy a family of four. But my method considerably reduces the volume of a chicken, and, since the meat is boneless, more is eaten. If you've got heavy eaters, you may need two fryers for a family of four. I might add that a person's size isn't always an indication of appetite. Our daughter, thin as a rail, has always eaten as much fried chicken or fish as a normal lumberjack.

chicken (fryers)	salt
peanut oil	pepper
flour (all-purpose)	

Apart from leading to tasty fried chicken, the above list is important not for what it contains but for what it leaves out. The recipe obviously doesn't have 22 secret spices to mess with. More importantly, it doesn't have egg or buttermilk and thick batter ingredients, such as breadcrumbs. My thinking is that eliminating the skin and thick batter does away with grease traps. But a batter, or bread-like coating of some sort, is needed simply because, if properly used on high heat, it prevents the meat from absorbing so much cooking oil.

I allow that I am fond of chicken fried skin and all, and, of course, my recipe will work with that method. For low-fat results, however, it's best to skin the chicken, keep the batter to a minimum, and fry it in a good vegetable oil. (Animal fat, such as beef suet or lard, contains lots of cholesterol.)

Skinned chicken seems to fry better if you will bone it

before frying. Boning the meat reduces the cooking time, makes for smaller pieces, and lowers the odds of inexperienced cooks putting chicken on the table that is brown on the outside and raw on the inside, as can (and does) happen with large pieces of bone-in breast. In fact, I usually cut the breast into fingers.

So, skin your chicken and bone it. Wash the meat. Salt and pepper each piece to taste. Roll each piece lightly in flour, or shake the batch in a small brown bag with flour. At this point, many cooks and cookbook writers recommended that the chicken be left out for a few minutes so that the batter will stick to the chicken. At one time, I did this, but I have changed my mind and find that I like the results better if the chicken is cooked almost immediately after flouring. Handle it carefully, however, during and after cooking so that the light coating of flour won't flake off.

If you are using an ordinary skillet, put about ½ to ¾ inch of peanut oil in it and bring it to heat before you start. I usually test the oil by touching a piece of floured chicken to it. If it sizzles nicely, I put several pieces into the skillet, then reduce the heat to medium. It's best to cook in several batches instead of overcrowding your frying pan. It's also important that each piece of chicken be drained properly before serving. This is best accomplished by laying each piece out on an ordinary brown paper bag. Spread the pieces out and avoid making a pile.

I always cook my chicken in an *uncovered* skillet, but many people do cover it up. A cover will reduce oil splatter, but, even so, I still don't recommend it. I don't want to be pinned down on this, but I'm certain that the sound and strength of the sizzle is an important part to sensing when the chicken is ready to turn or to take up. Also, I feel that covered chicken is partly steamed—which takes some of the crunch out of the fried batter. But this is just one man's opinion.

Another matter of opinion: cast-iron skillets cook better chicken than deep fryers, and can cook chicken in such a way that is difficult to duplicate with other techniques. The trick is to use just enough oil to cover about half of the chicken. In other words, each piece of chicken ought to touch the bottom of the cast-iron skillet, while the top of the piece ought to stick up out of the cooking oil. When the bottom is nicely browned, the piece is turned over and the other side is browned. Ideally, the chicken is turned only once. If all goes well, both the top and bottom of each piece of chicken will be browner than the sides simply because they were in direct contact with the cast iron. Thus, each piece of skillet-fried chicken offers a different crunch on top, bottom, and sides.

But cooking in a skillet is slow, and deep frying is really better suited for feeding lots of people. To be sure, toothsome chicken can be deep fried in a cast-iron pot of suitable depth, or in a Dutch oven. There is even a piece of cast-iron cookware called a chicken fryer. These are usually about 3 inches deep, as compared to 1½ or 2 inches for a frying pan, or 4 or 5 inches for a Dutch oven. There are also some cast-iron stew pots, fish fryers, and "French fry" pieces with a basket. All these can, of course, be used to fry chicken, and cast-iron washpots or other vats can be used at large outdoor cooking events. Indoors or out, however, large batch or small, I'll stick by the recipe above.

Just a few days after I had written the above text, one of my sons came in with a large wild turkey. We cut the breast into fingers, marinated it overnight in buttermilk, and then used the chicken finger recipe to cook it. Nothing was left. Two days later, we used the rest of the bird to make a gumbo. It was delicious.

Fried Fish

Except for large batch occasions, most of the fish that I eat are fried in a cast-iron skillet. My method and recipe are quite simple, similar in concept and philosophy to the fried chicken section above. I normally use only the following ingredients:

fish	peanut oil
white cornmeal, water-ground style	salt

The directions for fried chicken set forth above will work for skillet-fried fish. One important exception is that the peanut oil for frying fish should be as hot as possible without smoking. My reasons for using white cornmeal, peanut oil, and quick cooking times were set forth, in great detail, in my book *Good Vittles*, and they can't be repeated at full length here. Frying fish at high temperature in a skillet is a full-time job. I don't recommend that the skillet be covered, and this can cause grease to pop out. It can also cause fires. Be careful, and watch what you are doing.

In some ways, deep fryers are much easier to use, and of course some cast-iron cookware is made especially for frying fish. Dutch ovens, pots, and so on can also be used. All of these pieces, usually much deeper than a skillet, will do a very good job. But of course you'll have to use much more oil if you are going to deep fry, and this usually isn't practical for cooking for only two or three folks.

Many people fry fish on the patio these days, and portable gas-burning stoves are quite nice for this purpose; usually, these are nothing more than a gas burner mounted in a steady steel frame, made to support a container for holding lots of oil.

Of course, most cast-iron pots and Dutch ovens can be

used at a campfire to fry fish. Heat control is something of a problem, however, and often the best bet is to use a good skillet. Build a keyhole fire, designed to hold a frying pan steadily on the small end. When you are ready to cook, rake some coals into the small end and put the skillet over them. Pick it up and sit it down several times, making sure of a good balance. If the oil gets too hot, remove the pan for a few seconds. More coals can be added, as needed, during the cooking.

Some of the best fish I've ever tasted were cooked on a portable gas stove set up on the tailgate of a pickup truck, parked at streamside near a bridge. These were cooked in a 10½-inch cast-iron skillet. Some of the *worst* fish I've ever tried to eat were cooked on a similar stove in a large Dutch oven. The problem was that the stove wouldn't get the Dutch oven hot enough. The high sides and heavy metal acted as a heat sink, and the stove eye simply wouldn't do the job. As a result, the chef cooked the fish too long while trying to brown them. The long cooking dried the fish out, making them chewy and tough. They were small bluegills, one of the best of all fish, and they would have been delicious if fried quickly in a 10½-inch skillet. But of course some stoves and gas cookers will indeed heat large cookware and a gallon or more of oil. These are ideal if you've got a lot of folks to feed on the patio or under the bridge.

Although sometimes a so-called fish fryer comes complete with a lid, I would advise you to leave it off in most cases. For one thing, you'll miss out on the reassuring sizzle of frying fish, the aroma, and the visual contact that tells you when the fish is brown enough to take up. Usually, a fish fried in deep oil should be taken up soon after it floats, which you can't see if you've got a lid on the cooker. On the other hand, if you're frying fish during a dust storm or a mayfly rise, maybe a lid will help.

Cowboy Cooking

The first time that I really sat up and took notice of cowboy cooking was in the reading room of the public library in a small town in southern Alabama. While I was glancing through a cookbook, a blackened spot on one of the pages jumped out and caught my eye. Quickly I thumbed back until I found the spot and saw that someone had inked out part of the recipe's name and had printed in "Southern" where another word ought to have been. I might add that this wasn't a casual X-out. It was a most thorough ink job, done with the aid of a free-flowing pen. I say this with confidence because the paper did not seem to have had pressure on it from a regular ball point.

I figure, further, that a ruler or some straight edge was used, such as a library card. Because the ink job was so well done, so precise and economical of rectangle, it took some detective work for me to put the name back together again. Ironically, the neatness of the rectangle helped me to extrapolate the word, just as the inkout had drawn me there in the first place. I had no calipers or em-scale, but, by comparing with the eye the black rectangle with the letters around it, I determined that the word probably had 11 characters. As you can clearly see in the scale diagram below, the word "southern" on the left or the configuration of letters simply doesn't neatly fill out the block, as you will see if you will compare its length to the others. Further, the mystery word was not made up entirely of short letters, such as 's' or 'n' or 'a,' and did *not* contain any letters that jutted down, such as 'p' or 'g' or 'y,' as shown on the right side of the diagram below. The word had to contain some letters that stuck up above the center line, such as 'b' and 't' and 'h.' After an exhaustive search in Webster's, I concluded, at least to my own satisfaction, that the term, "son-of-a-bitch," as highlighted in the middle of the diagram below, is the only word or term in the English language that fits.

southern	son-of-a-bitch	pineyigiyiquip
southern	son-of-a-bitch	pineyigiyiquip

I might add that the name of the recipe was also altered in the book's index, by the same hand. I'm no Sherlock Holmes, but this fact, I think, narrows the list of suspects to include only those few people who know that some books have indexes—and who have time to fix dirty words in books. In any case, whoever made the mark is guilty of defacing public property and destroying historical records. It's an authentic cowboy recipe, and cowboys were frequent users of the term "son of a bitch" and its adjectival form, "son-of-a-bitch." I have therefore corrected the recipe in the library for the benefit of the Henry County Historical Society.

After the correction was made, one of the members of the Library Board complained, at a City Council meeting, that too many high school students were frequenting the public library. The students took up too much of the librarians' time, it was said. What do you make of that, Watson? Time from doing what?

In any case, son-of-a-bitch stew was cooked on the range, where the cowboys often dressed out a steer for eating purposes. My guess is that they would almost always select a young steer, partly because they didn't need a big one and partly because a young one would make better eating when freshly killed. They made son-of-a-bitch stew with the so-called variety meats, including a part of the animal called the marrow gut. This is the conduit that connects the two stomachs of ruminants, or cud-chewing animals, such as cows and camels. The marrow gut is very, very good when taken from young animals that have not yet been weaned.

If for culinary or historical reasons you want to try the recipe, here's what you'll need:

2 pounds calf stew meat	1½ pounds calf liver
1 set calf brains	salt
1 set calf marrow gut	pepper
1 set calf sweetbreads	Tabasco or other hot pepper
½ a calf heart	sauce

Cut the meat, heart, and liver into 1-inch cubes. Clean the marrow gut and cut it into rings. Put the cubed meat, heart, and marrow gut into a large Dutch oven or cast-iron pot and cover with water. Bring to boil, reduce heat, cover with a lid, and simmer for 2 or 3 hours. Add salt, pepper, and hot sauce to taste. Cut the brains and sweetbreads into 1-inch cubes and add to the stew. Simmer for another hour, but do not boil after adding the brains and sweetbreads.

Omit the marrow gut if you don't have any at hand, or don't have a hankering for it. On the other hand, if you're feeling frisky, you may want to add the mountain oysters, cubed, along with the other choice cuts. Feeds 10 to 12.

Chuck Wagon Biscuits

Although sourdough and other bread can be baked in a Dutch oven, on a stovetop, or at a camp fire, my guess is that cowboys on the move ate more fried biscuits because they were easier to cook. They usually had milk, flour, and cooking oil (or shortening) available, but such ingredients as chicken eggs might have been hard to come by and didn't travel well on a chuck wagon. The following recipe can be made with either a Dutch oven or a large skillet (I prefer the latter) and it may come in handy in camp—where you might well have some sour milk on hand. Cultured buttermilk powder works fine if it is properly mixed.

2½ cups all-purpose flour
cooking oil
2 teaspoons salt

1 heaping teaspoon baking soda
1 cup buttermilk or sour milk

Mix flour, salt, and soda. Add ⅓ cup of cooking oil, cutting it in, as the womenfolks say. Shape mixture into an oval and make a well in the middle with your fist. Pour in the buttermilk and stir it until the dough comes together. Flour a smooth surface and knead the dough for 10 or 15 strokes. (Don't get carried away and knead the dough too long.)

Pour about an inch of cooking oil into a large skillet and heat it. While the oil is heating, pinch off biscuit-sized balls of dough and flatten them a little. Fry the biscuits for 2 or 3 minutes on each side. Drain on a flattened brown bag or other absorbent paper. Eat while hot. The above measures make about 30 biscuits. If you don't have cowboys to feed, cut the measures in half.

Cornbread in the Skillet

Owing to its even heating and non-stick properties, a well-seasoned cast-iron skillet or griddle cooks wonderful cornbreads on top of the stove or in the oven. I prefer a griddle for cooking the thin, flat breads, but a skillet will work nicely for most cornbreads. Be sure to try the recipes below.

Johnnycakes

The New England colonists made very good use of the corn that they got from the American Indians. Cornmeal johnnycakes, buttered and eaten with maple syrup, became traditional fare. Actually, they were first called journeycakes, simply because they rode well and were standard fare on a trip before motels and fast-food outlets lined our trails. There are a thousand variations, but here's a good basic recipe:

2½ cups yellow cornmeal, fine
2 large chicken eggs
2 tablespoons lard (or other shortening)
1 cup whole milk
1 cup water
1 teaspoon salt

In a bowl, beat the eggs slightly, then stir in the water and milk. Mix in the cornmeal. In a 10-inch cast-iron skillet, melt the lard, pour it into the bowl, and stir in well with the cornmeal mixture. (Leave a little lard in the skillet, spreading it to cover all the bottom and sides.) Heat the greased skillet, then pour ¼ cup of cornmeal mixture into it. Spread it thin, like a pancake. The thickness should be about ¼ inch. Cook the johnnycake for 3 or 4 minutes. Turn and cook the other side for 3 minutes. Repeat until all the batter is used up. Serve the bread with a meal, or butter each johnnycake and top it with maple syrup.

A similar bread, sometimes called hoecake, became traditional in parts of the south. It was often made with white meal mixed with water and a little salt. Thick cane syrup was usually eaten with it instead of maple syrup, and of course many farms had their own cane mills. If you want hoecake instead of johnnycakes, use my recipe for griddle bread (below). Butter the bread and eat it with sugar cane syrup. I might add that there is much confusion about what's what, and some people call corn pone hoecake, partly because the pones are about the size of your hand, just the right size for cooking on the blade of a hoe.

Griddle Bread

Here's a thin bread that is best cooked on a griddle in the oven. It's easy to make—and it's very good.

white cornmeal (fine stone-ground)	salt and pepper
hot water	cooking oil

Put about two cups of cornmeal into a mixing bowl and stir in some boiling hot water until you get a rather thin batter. Salt and pepper to taste. Let the mixture sit for 10 minutes or longer, during which time it will become a little firmer. Carefully add hot water until the mixture gets as thin as pancake batter.

Grease the griddle and heat it. Pour batter into the center of the griddle and quickly spread it evenly to the edges. Don't pour in too much batter, as the bread should be no more than ½ inch thick. Cook on medium heat until the bottom starts to brown. Flip the bread over and cook the other side until it starts to brown and the bread seems firm enough to turn. The trick is to flip the bread without breaking it. My wife claims that somebody in her family can flip the bread over with a quick push-and-pull motion to the griddle, but I've never seen any proof of this. I can usually turn the bread with two large spatulas, one on top and one underneath, well coordinated.

Note: This griddle bread can also be cooked in a hot oven. Merely grease the griddle with bacon grease, spread the bread mixture in it, and bake until browned.

Cross Creek Crackling Bread

When I make crackling bread, I merely add a handful of cracklings to my simple cornpone or griddle bread recipe. But recipes abound, and you may want to try the one below, which I have adapted from Marjorie Kinnan Rawlings' *Cross Creek Cookery.* This recipe, she says, turns "po' folks' cornbread in the autumn into a delicacy unobtainable in high places." I agree. She set the recipe in the fall of the year because that is hog killing time in rural areas, when cracklings are rendered (as described under the next heading). Here's what you'll need:

2 cups fine white cornmeal, water-ground style	½ cup good cracklings ½ cup skim milk

½ cup water
1 chicken egg
3 tablespoons baking
  powder

1 teaspoon salt

Preheat the oven to 400 degrees and grease a 10-inch cast-iron skillet. Mix cornmeal, baking powder, and salt in a bowl. Add the water and skim milk. Stir until you have a smooth mixture. Stir in the egg and cracklings. Put the mixture into the greased skillet and bake it for about 30 minutes.

The size of the cracklings makes a difference. As Mrs. Rawlings says, "If the cracklings are no larger than a pea, I stir them in whole. Otherwise, I break up the larger pieces. Some cooks crush the cracklings with a rolling pin, but this makes them too fine for my taste. There is no point in having cracklings, and then disguising them." Mrs. Rawlings also noted that cracklin' bread is a far cry from the "shortening bread" made famous by the song. Frankly, I'll have to admit that I don't really know what shortening bread is. I've never eaten anything that was called by that name by the cook who made it. According to Jessica B. Harris's *Iron Pots and Wooden Spoons*, shortening bread was made with butter, flour, brown sugar, and a little salt—and she lists it as a dessert, not a bread. Maybe that's why mama's little baby loves shortenin' bread, shortenin' bread. I rest my case. For the time being.

How to Make Cracklings

Many people, including some cookbook writers who ought to know better, believe that cracklings are pork skins, or rinds, that have been cooked down in the process of rendering lard. It's true that cracklings may contain some skin or rind, but it's also true that cracklings do not necessarily have to contain any skin at all. In fact, the best ones often don't. Too much skin, improperly handled, can ruin crackling bread, making it or part of it chewy, like greasy leather.

To make cracklings at hog killing time, the fat is trimmed away from the various parts. Some of this fat has no skin attached to it; in fact, most of the hog's skin is left on the hams, shoulders, jowls, and slabs of bacon. What's left of the skin is sometimes cut up with chunks of fat and put into the lard pot. But it can also be cut off the fat and discarded or perhaps set aside for later use as fried "pork skins" or, maybe, for bass fishing lures.

In any case, the fat is cut into chunks, with or without skin, before it is put into the lard pot. The best cracklings will result from small chunks no larger than an inch. Even smaller chunks are better—especially if they contain skin. The fat is then heated in a large pot, usually a cast-iron wash pot, until the lard is rendered. The residue of each chunk of fat will float to the top. After further cooking, it will then sink to the bottom. It's best to get each crackling just before it sinks, but of course it's impossible to get the whole batch at exactly the right time. Larger pieces will take a little longer. Also, it's best to stir the pot with a paddle from time to time so that the bottom won't get ready before the middle. After the cracklings are skimmed from the lard, or strained out, they are spread on a table or other surface to drain. If all has gone well, each crackling will be about the size of a #1 buckshot, and will be crisp and dry. If the cracklings contain skin, it should be crunchy but not hard or leathery.

Cracklings are sometimes available in meat markets, but

usually these are too large for making good bread. Break them up. If the skins are leathery, throw them out.

If you want to make some cracklings, but don't plan to kill hogs anytime soon, get 10 or 12 pounds of good pork fat from your butcher or meat processor. Tell him that you want it for rendering lard and making cracklings. Cut it into small pieces and cook it slowly in a cast-iron Dutch oven for several hours, stirring from time to time. Take up the cracklings when they are brown and crisp. Drain them on brown paper bags.

Save the lard. When it cools, put it into wide-mouth jars and store it in a cool place. Use it in old recipes that call for "shortening" or lard. I'm no bakery expert, but some good cooks say that pork lard is necessary for making some of our more dainty pastries.

I refrigerate cracklings (and lard), but, frankly, I don't think you'll have much of a storage problem if you'll make a batch of crackling bread. I've made two batches in one day, and, in fact, I can make a meal of it if I've got some good cold buttermilk. Call it soul food, joke about it as being "poor white trash cooking," or make a jingle about shortenin' bread, shortenin' bread—better yet, shut up and pass the platter my way!

Jalapeño Bread

Here's a tasty recipe that I like with Brunswick stew and somewhat bland casseroles made with whole kernel corn.

3 cups fine yellow cornmeal	3 chicken eggs
2 cups buttermilk	¼ cup peanut oil
6 or 8 fresh Jalapeño	1 teaspoon salt
peppers	
1 large onion	

Grease a large, well-seasoned cast-iron skillet and preheat the oven to 375 degrees. Slice the Jalapeño peppers in half lengthwise and remove the seeds. Then mince the peppers. (Many chefs will brown the peppers under a broiler or on a hot skillet first, then peel them. I don't do this, but suit yourself.) Peel the onion and grate it. When you get through crying, mix the meal, buttermilk, and oil. Break and whisk the chicken eggs, then mix them into the batter, along with the peppers, onion, and salt. Dump this mixture into a large cast-iron skillet. Pat the top with oil and then bake the bread in the center of the oven for 40 minutes, or until the surface is slightly browned. Turn the skillet over onto a plate, and the bread will come out without sticking every time.

This cast-iron pan bakes bread in convenient pie-shaped pieces.

This bread and similar yellow-meal breads are sometimes made in a special cast-iron pan with 6 or 8 pie-shaped cavities. These pans work fine, especially when you want neat pieces of bread that require no cutting and that hold together well. Usually, half the above recipe will fill one of these bread pans.

Livingston Perfect

I don't want to overwork skillet breads and other cornmeal products, but, on the other hand, I feel that I owe this recipe and technique to my readers simply because it's the best. I don't often make exact measures for cornbread, mixing, instead, by feel and adding either meal or water until I get the right consistency. Nonetheless, I worked out the meal-to-water measures below and added some finely diced salt pork. The results are outstanding. One word of caution, however. Ideal measures may depend in part on the kind of cornmeal you have, and whether it be extra-fine, medium, or what not. Adjustments in the meal may be necessary.

2 cups fine-ground white cornmeal
2½ cups boiling water
1½ tablespoon peanut oil

¾ cup crisp salt pork, diced
½ teaspoon salt

Preheat the oven to 400 degrees. Finely dice some salt pork in a 10-inch skillet, then fry it until it is crisp. Cook enough to yield ¾ cup. Drain the diced pieces and discard the oil that cooked out of the salt pork. In a bowl, mix the meal, water, salt, and fried salt pork. Let sit for 15 minutes. Put 1½ tablespoons peanut oil in the skillet, coating the bottom and sides. Put the meal mixture into the skillet and place it into the center of the oven. Cook for 30 or 40 minutes, or until the cornbread has a crispy crust on the sides and on the top. During the last 10 minutes of cooking, brush the top of the bread with oil to help it brown properly.

Cooking Cajun

Cajun dishes, for some reason or another, just seem to come out better in cast iron.
—The Frank Davis Seafood Notebook

Cajun cooking and Creole cooking, if there is a difference, have gotten into a mess over the years. I'm not going to straighten it out, even if I thought that I could. The Cajuns might blame the rest of the country for corrupting this recipe or that, but the problem is really with the Cajuns themselves. While the general reader wants for definition, so as to know what's what, you can find cookbooks, written by Cajuns or at least by people in lower Louisiana, that contain hundreds of recipes for jambalayas having neither ham nor rice in them, and just as many recipes for gumbos without okra.

For example, I recently counted seven gumbo recipes from Justin Wilson's *Gourmet and Gourmand Cookbook,* and more than half of these don't have okra listed in the ingredients. Without okra, some of these dishes could just have easily been called soup, stew, goulash, or, yes, jambalaya. Wilson no doubt cooks better than he talks, and talks better than he spells and writes, and I suppose he has got license to do pretty much what he wants to do with language or food and call it Cajun.

Moreover, Paul Prudhomme's *Louisiana Kitchen* has lots of

gumbo recipes listed and, again, more than half of them contained no okra at all. I confess that I haven't looked deeply or even widely into the matter, and don't intend to do so simply because I've seen all that I want to see. In fact, I hereby wash my hands of the mess, but I must say, before moving on, that I have noticed that Cajun cookbooks have lots of cast-iron cookware pieces in the photographs! The authors may talk about zapping out a roux in a microwave oven, or in a thin Teflon-coated pan, but when it gets down to Cajun on Cajun, they'll reach for cast iron every time.

Jambalaya

A cast-iron frying pan with a large diameter (13 inches or so) and a cover works best for jambalaya, but the dish can also be made in a Dutch oven. Jambalaya should have ham and rice in it, but the other ingredients can, and do, vary from one batch to the next. Here's what I recommend for openers:

1 cup long grain rice, uncooked
1 pound smoke-cured ham
2 pounds chicken breasts
6 slices bacon
1 cup chicken broth, hot
1 can tomatoes (16-ounce size)
8 ounces fresh mushrooms, whole
1 stalk celery, chopped with leaves

1 large onion, diced
1 green pepper, diced
½ teaspoon thyme
1 teaspoon salt
½ teaspoon black pepper
1 tablespoon Worcestershire sauce
Tabasco sauce to taste

Fry the bacon in a large skillet until crisp and set it aside on a brown paper bag to drain. Cut the ham into chunks. Skin and bone the chicken breast; cut the meat into chunks. Brown the meat in the bacon drippings, take it up, and set it aside to drain with the bacon. Add the rice to the bacon drippings in the skillet and cook on low until it starts to brown. Add the onions, celery, mushrooms, and green pepper. Sauté on low heat for 8 minutes. Chop the canned tomatoes and add them to the skillet, along with the juice. Add the chicken broth. Put the chicken, ham, and crumbled bacon into the skillet. Stir in the thyme, salt, black pepper, and Worcestershire sauce. Bring to heat, cover tightly, reduce heat, and simmer for 30 minutes. About 10 minutes before serving, taste for seasoning. Add Tabasco sauce to taste, along with more salt if needed. Let sit for a few minutes before serving. Feeds 8.

Variations: Substitute alligator meat or turtle for chicken. Add other vegetables, in modest amounts, if you have them at hand and need to clean out the refrigerator. Also, remember that many people like sausage in their jambalaya instead of ham. Try it.

Seafood Gumbo

I've eaten a hundred very good gumbo dishes that were made without the aid of a roux of any sort, and they tasted fine. But as I gain experience I realize more and more that the color of a truly outstanding seafood gumbo starts with a dark roux. Making a roux can be almost ritualistic—or one can be zapped out in a microwave oven. Long, slow cooking in cast iron produces the best color, however, if it is stirred and watched and handled with tender loving care.

One of my favorite seafood gumbo recipes is made with the aid of a cast-iron skillet and a stovetop Dutch oven. Here's what you'll need:

FOR A DUTCH OVEN ROUX:

½ cup cooking oil   6 tablespoons flour

Put the cooking oil into the Dutch oven and stir in the flour on very low heat. A good dark roux will take an hour or longer. To be sure, the roux will darken quicker if you will turn up the heat, but if you've got the time, it's best to go slow. If you use more heat, be sure to stir the roux constantly with a wooden spoon. If you go slower, stir from time to time while preparing the vegetables, peeling the shrimp, etc., as required for the steps below.

When the roux has browned, add the following to the Dutch oven:

1½ quarts boiling water   1 pound smoke-cured ham
1½ quarts chicken broth   hocks

Bring the liquid to a light boil, then reduce heat, cover, and cook for an hour or so. When the ham hocks are tender, remove them and pull the meat off the bones. Discard fat, skin, and bones. Chop the meat, put it back into the Dutch oven, cover, and simmer.

FOR A CAST-IRON SKILLET:

2 pounds fresh okra, cut   2 bell peppers, seeded and
   into ½-inch segments   chopped
2 large onions, chopped   1 cup fresh parsley,
4 cloves garlic, minced   chopped
3 stalks celery, scraped and   ½ cup bacon drippings
   chopped

Heat the bacon drippings in the skillet. Sauté the okra for a few minutes, then add the other vegetables. Sauté for about 20 minutes on low heat. Then add vegetables to the Dutch oven, along with the following:

INTO THE DUTCH OVEN:

2 quarts fresh tomatoes,
   peeled and diced
1 tablespoon salt
½ teaspoon red pepper
   flakes
½ teaspoon black pepper

1 teaspoon thyme
2 tablespoons
   Worcestershire sauce
4 bay leaves

Add tomatoes and seasonings to the Dutch oven, stir, and bring to a light bubble. Reduce heat, cover tightly, and simmer for at least two hours, stirring a couple of times. While waiting, peel the shrimp, shuck the oysters, and pick the crabs.

LATE ADDITIONS:

2 pounds peeled shrimp
1 pound crab meat
1 pint fresh oysters (with
   part of salty juice)

filé
rice (cooked separately)

Increase the Dutch oven heat to high. Add shrimp, crab meat, and oysters. Cook for 6 or 7 minutes, or until the shrimp turn pink and the oysters curl on the edges. Take the gumbo off the heat, then test for seasonings. Stir in a pinch of filé to thicken the gumbo. Go easy here; too much filé will ruin your dish. If you don't have experience with this stuff (which is nothing more than powdered sassafras leaves), you might prefer to add the filé to individual servings instead of to the whole batch.

Many folks serve gumbo over rice, but I prefer to ladle a serving of gumbo into a bowl, then add rice with a large spoon. This method gives the individual more control, and works especially well with filé added to each serving. In other words, stir in the filé before you add the rice. Feeds 10 or 12.

Rabbit Sauce Piquante

People in south Louisiana eat lots of rabbits, or think they do. In addition to domestic rabbits, they have native cottontails, small marsh rabbits, and larger swamp rabbits. Also, muskrats are sold in some quarters under the name "marsh rabbit." In any case, here's a dish that I make with the aid of a 14-inch jambalaya skillet and a stovetop Dutch oven.

THE MEAT:

2 domestic rabbits, or 3 cottontails	juice of 1 lemon
	salt
1 cup peanut oil	pepper
1 cup beef broth	

Skin the rabbits, bone the meat, and cut it into 1-inch cubes. Sprinkle the meat with the juice of 1 lemon and let it sit for an hour. Sprinkle the meat with salt and pepper. Heat a cup of peanut oil in a Dutch oven and brown the meat slightly on medium high heat. Pour off grease, add beef broth, bring to boil, reduce heat, cover, and simmer for 30 minutes.

FOR ROUX AND SAUCE:

½ cup cooking oil
6 tablespoons flour
1 large onion, chopped
1 stalk celery, chopped

1 bell pepper, chopped
1 can tomato sauce (8-ounce size)
¼ cup white wine vinegar
1 cup water

While the rabbit meat is simmering in the Dutch oven, make a roux in a large skillet by heating the cooking oil and stirring in the flour. Cook and stir until you have a brown roux. (Start the roux while the rabbit meat is being marinated with the lemon juice.) Add the water, white wine vinegar, tomato sauce, bell pepper, celery, and onion. Let simmer for 15 minutes. Add the rabbit pieces.

LATE ADDITIONS:

3 cloves garlic, minced
¼ cup parsley, chopped

2 green onions with tops, finely chopped
rice (cooked separately)

Sprinkle the dish with minced garlic, parsley, and green onion tops. Stir. Simmer uncovered for 15 minutes. Serve over rice. Feeds 4 to 6.

Mexican Cooking, Cast-Iron Style

Before the Spanish and the French arrived, native Mexican cooking no doubt developed with the aid of earthenware pots, and possibly heated flat rocks. The tortilla, for example, was probably first cooked on a flat rock. And chili was probably stewed in an olla, which would require long, slow cooking. Another speculation: pinto beans were cooked in an olla for long hours, and leftover beans were mashed up and warmed on a hot flat rock, making the original *frijoles refritos*. In any case, I find that a cast-iron griddle (or skillet) does a great job on tortillas, and cast-iron Dutch ovens or pots work nicely on slow-cooked chili.

Chili

The term *chili con carne* means pepper with meat. Thus, any meat cooked down with chili peppers, or with powder made primarily with dried and ground hot chili peppers, would be the real stuff. Over the years, two other native Mexican ingredients—beans and tomatoes—were naturally added in one way or another. Some modern Americans even assume that chili has beans in it. I suggest that you cook the beans separately, then add them to the chili bowls for those who want them, or serve them as a side dish.

Other grounds for chili arguments arise over the kind of meat. Some want ground meat; others want the meat cut

90

into chunks. Personally, I prefer the chunks, or a mixture. I also like a mixture of meats, as, for example, part venison and part lean pork or javelina. (For convenience, the recipe below calls for pork and beef.)

Chili profits from long, slow cooking, and I think that a cast-iron pot or Dutch oven is ideal.

2 pounds lean beef, trimmed and cubed
1 pound fresh pork, trimmed and cubed
6 slices bacon
1 can tomato sauce (12-ounce size)
1 large onion, chopped
3 cloves garlic, minced
1 large bell pepper, chopped
2 Jalapeño peppers, seeded and minced
2 tablespoons prepared chili powder
1 teaspoon salt
½ teaspoon cumin seed, crushed
½ teaspoon dried oregano leaves
2 cups beef broth

In a Dutch oven, fry the bacon until crisp. Put the bacon on a brown paper bag to drain. Crumble when cool. In the bacon drippings, brown the diced beef and pork, stirring in the onion, garlic, and bell pepper. Add the beef broth, chili powder, jalapeño peppers, salt, cumin seeds, and oregano. Stir in the tomato sauce. Bring to boil. Reduce heat to very low, cover, and simmer for 4 or 5 hours. Add a little water from time to time, if needed. Note, however, that this particular recipe was designed to be on the thick side. Serve it in a bowl with crackers and pinto beans (cooked separately). Also, try a handful of chopped onion (chilled) on top of each bowl. Or, roll some freshly made, hot tortillas and dunk them into the chili. Feeds 6 to 8.

Some Mexican food experts bake or roast Jalapeño peppers until the skin cracks. Then they peel them, cut them in half, seed them, and use them as needed. This might add something to, say, a stuffed pepper snack, but I think it is a waste of time for a dish like chili that is to be cooked for hours.

> *Remember that chili just doesn't taste right if you don't cook it in an iron pot. I suppose a little of the iron leaches out in the chili and provides that little extra push it needs.*
> —Linda West Eckhardt's *The Only Texas Cookbook*

Texas Chili

Be warned that the recipe above has a strong, thick tomato base. You may also want to try another recipe, without any kind of tomato ingredient. I call the recipe below Texas chili, but, frankly, it's hard to tell where Texas quits and Mexico starts.

3 pounds ground beef (lean)	**6 tablespoons chili powder**
½ cup cooking oil	**1 teaspoon cumin seed,**
2 large onions, chopped	**crushed**
3 cloves garlic, minced	**6 cups beef stock**
	salt and pepper to taste

In a Dutch oven, heat the oil and sauté the onions and garlic for 5 minutes, then take them up with a large spoon. Brown the ground beef, then pour off the oil from the Dutch oven. Return the onions and garlic. Add beef stock, chili powder, and cumin seeds. Stir and bring to boil. Reduce heat, cover, and simmer for at least an hour. Add a little salt to taste. Add pepper if needed. Simmer for a few more minutes and serve. Feeds 6 to 8.

Tortillas

Once I rode across the Rio Grande on a donkey to a small Mexican village. The aroma of good food filled the air, but, to be honest, I didn't see a peasant woman patting out perfectly round tortillas with the palms of her hands. I've tried it myself, and it did not take me long to determine that, in this matter, practice would not make perfect. Fortunately, however, hand patting isn't necessary; anyone can press out a few for home use with the aid of two sheets of wax paper and a flat-bottom pie plate, as directed below. If you plan to put up a taco stand in a busy place, however, you would profit by having a mechanical tortilla press.

Some books about Mexican foods specify tamalina or masa harina, which is sometimes available in places that traffic in Mexican ingredients. I use ordinary white stone-ground cornmeal, fine grind, from the grocery store. It should, however, be very fine, like flour. Some of the coarse yellow meals simply won't work, and any meal, white, yellow, or blue, that contains the words "self-rising" should be avoided. What you need is ground corn, with nothing put into it—or taken away from it.

2 cups white cornmeal, fine stone ground	1 cup boiling hot water

Mix the cornmeal and the water, making a stiff dough. Shape the dough into balls, using about 1½ tablespoons per ball. (The above measures should make 12 tortillas.) Set the dough balls aside while you heat a cast-iron griddle (or large skillet) on medium heat. Do not grease the griddle or spray it with no-stick stuff.

Tear off some squares of waxed paper. Put one square on a flat, smooth surface. Put a dough ball in the center. Center another piece of wax paper on top of the dough ball. Position a pie plate over the dough and press straight down. The dough will spread out to a circle of about 6 inches in diameter, and to a thickness of about ⅛ inch. How hard do you press? This is easy, once you get the hang of it. Start with a clear Pyrex pie plate and you can watch the dough spread!

When the griddle is hot, carefully remove the top sheet of wax paper and flip the uncooked tortilla over onto the surface of the griddle. Carefully remove the wax paper. Cook for a couple of minutes. Turn and cook the other side for two minutes.

For best results, stack the tortillas and keep them hot until you are ready to eat. Mexicans will turn a bowl over them to hold in the heat, and it is also common practice to cover them with a wet, steaming hot cloth on a warmed plate or platter. If they will be eaten right away, a basket covered with a napkin will do. If the tortillas get cold and somewhat dry, they can be sprinkled lightly with water and reheated before serving.

With the tortillas you can make tacos or enchiladas or other Mexican specialties. Or you can eat it like bread. First, melt a little butter. Then roll a tortilla, hold it like a bundle between your fingers, dip the end into the melted butter, and take a bite. Repeat the process. When eating tortillas this way, I like a little salt in the butter.

Corn Chips After you cook a batch of tortillas, cut them into strips about ½ inch wide and 2 inches long. Heat 1 inch of peanut oil in a skillet. Carefully put a dozen or so of the strips into the hot oil. Fry until browned, which will take only a minute. Take up and place on a brown paper bag to drain. Salt lightly. Repeat the procedure until all the tortilla strips have been fried. Serve while hot, or warm.

Tostados The corn chips described above are intended to be eaten by themselves. If you have dip or meat sauce, follow the directions for corn chips, but cut the tortillas into triangles before frying.

Taco Shells Heat ½ inch of peanut oil in a skillet. Using tongs, place one tortilla into the hot oil. Carefully hold one edge of the tortilla with the tongs, lift it out of the oil slightly, and fold it over until you form the shape of a taco shell. Hold it in this position until the bottom half cooks and is crisp. Turn the taco over with the tongs and cook the other half until it is crisp.

Flour Tortillas

Some folks prefer flour tortillas to those made of cornmeal, and a number of recipes call for them. Here's a good recipe to try on your griddle:

2 cups white flour	½ teaspoon salt
2 tablespoons lard	warm water

In a bowl, mix flour and salt. Cut in the lard, then slowly mix in enough warm water to make a soft dough; usually, a tad over ½ cup will be about right. Let the dough sit for 20 minutes, then divide it into 8 or 9 balls of equal size. Dust a smooth surface with a little flour and roll the balls out. The dough should be at least 8 inches in diameter, and about ⅛ inch thick. (Usually, you can find a bowl top or some dish that will be about the right diameter; this can be used to help cut the dough in a circle.) One at a time, carefully place the flat dough rounds on a heated ungreased griddle. Cook for 1½ to 2 minutes on each side, turning carefully with a pancake spatula. Do not brown either side.

Stack the tortillas on a warm surface and wrap them with a warm, slightly damp cloth until you are ready to serve them, or to use them as an ingredient in other recipes.

'49er and Sourdough Cooking

Cast-iron skillets were fastened to the backs of covered wagons and carried along when families heeded the advice, "Go West!" The '49ers loaded their black iron and headed out to California to find their fortunes in gold, and many of the miners used small skillets to pan for gold when they got there.

—Diana Becker Finlay

The '49ers, and, a little later, the Alaskan camp cooks who became known as "sourdoughs," had to make do in remote areas. Even if their grub stake was large, transportation and replenishment was a problem. I'm sure that they made use of native fruits, berries, and greens in season, as well as available fish and game. As I see it, however, these men were too busy looking for gold to waste much time foraging for food. Bread was their sustenance. To make it, they used a sourdough starter, which was kept from one batch to another. I'm sure that they baked loaves of bread and batches of biscuits from time to time, especially when the cabin was snowed under, but I feel that the flapjack was what they cooked more often than not. Just the other night, I was reading a pamphlet called "An Illinois Gold Hunter in the Black Hills," written in 1876, and the author, Jerry Bryan, made several references to what he called "'49er Slapjacks."

Sourdough breads can still be made in camp, or at home. There must be a thousand sourdough recipes, but all of them have one thing in common: a starter. Most modern people who make sourdough breads save the starter from one batch to the next, partly because sourdough is believed to improve with age. If you lose your starter, you'll have to borrow some from a neighbor in the next wagon, or you'll have to start from scratch. Good starters can be made from potatoes as well as from sour milk, and of course many recipes and procedures can be found. Some practitioners make a ritual of sourdough, and insist on making a first batch of starter to sweeten the crock; then they throw it away and make a second batch in the same crock. While one starter may not be quite as good as another, too much depends on other conditions, such as temperature and humidity, for cabin cooks to get the same taste year after year. In short, most modern cooks will come out just as good by using dry yeast to make a starter. Of course, dry yeast is available in small packages at any grocery store. Here's a recipe that's easy to remember:

Sourdough Starter

1 package dry yeast (¼- 2 cups flour
ounce envelope)
2 cups lukewarm water

Sift your flour if it has got weevils in it. Heat some water until it is warm to the touch, about like milk for babies. In a glass or crockery container, slowly mix all the ingredients and beat well. Cover with a piece of cheesecloth or clean sheeting. Let the starter stand in a warm place for 48 hours. (Do not use aluminum foil or plastic film to cover the starter, and do not keep it in a closed cabinet.) Stir the starter every 8 hours or so. As the starter ferments, bubbles will form, the mixture will rise somewhat, and the characteristic sour smell will develop. After 48 hours, the starter (called a sponge when it is ready to use) can be kept in the refrigerator. A clear liquid may gather on top of the sponge. Stir it back in before using the starter.

After you remove a cup of starter for a recipe, replace it with a fresh batch of flour and water. (No additional yeast is necessary.) Merely mix equal parts of flour and warm water, then stir a cup of the mixture into the remaining starter. Cover the new starter with a cloth and leave it in a warm place for about 10 hours. Then refrigerate it until you are ready to cook more sourdough bread, biscuits, or pancakes. It's best to add new flour and water to the starter once a week. After adding new flour and water, let the starter sit in a warm place for a day or so.

In the method above, several cups of starter are kept at hand, ready to use. Some people, I might add, hold out only a cup of starter, and they mix all of it into a new batch, forming a sponge, the night before cooking with it. Then a cup of the sponge is held back for a starter.

Sourdough Biscuits

I haven't seen a lard can lately, but when I was growing up they were commonly used around the house and farm. If I remember correctly, they held about 5 gallons. Back then, lard was a very popular oil for cooking. But, alas, it is high in cholesterol and has been replaced, on supermarket shelves, almost entirely by vegetable oils.

The old chuckwagon cooks used lots of lard, as well as oil

rendered from salt pork, for baking sourdough breads. But in some remote camps, such as those set up by the mountain men, some of the '49ers, and the "sourdough" cooks of Alaska, lard was sometimes hard to come by. They no doubt substituted other animal fats, and lard made from bear fat was highly regarded. For the record, I'll add that the lightest biscuits I've ever eaten were made with goose grease substituted for the lard in the recipe below. If you don't have hog lard or goose grease, use vegetable shortening or oil, as well as butter, margarine, or bacon drippings.

1 cup sourdough starter (see recipe above)
1 cup flour
¼ cup lard

1½ teaspoons sugar
1 teaspoon baking powder
¼ teaspoon salt

In a large bowl, mix the flour, sugar, baking powder, and salt. Then cut in the lard or other shortening. This can be accomplished with a pastry blender. If you don't have one of these, try working two knives in a criss-cross manner. When you finish, the pastry should resemble bread crumbs. Form a hole in the center of this mixture and pour the cup of sourdough starter into it. Stir the starter with a wooden spoon until all of the flour mixture has been mixed into the starter. Place a handful of flour on a smooth surface and spread it out evenly. Turn the dough out of the bowl onto the flour surface and knead it a few times to make the dough smooth. Do not knead very long, as working it will produce a tough biscuit. Pat the dough gently down to a thickness of about ¾ inch. Grease the bottom and about half the sides of your Dutch oven lightly. Break off pieces of the biscuit dough, about the size of a golf ball, and place them into the Dutch oven. I like for mine to touch, which will produce fluffy pull-apart biscuits. (Your Dutch oven will hold more of these. If you want thinner, crisper biscuits, make the dough ½-inch thick and cut the biscuits out with a biscuit cutter or jar mouth.) Sit the Dutch oven in a warm, draft-free place for 10 minutes so that the dough can rise a little. If you are in camp on a cold night, sit the Dutch oven beside the fire, but not too close, and turn it around after 5 minutes.

While the biscuits are rising, mix 1 cup of flour and 1 cup of warm water. Stir this into your starter so that you will be ready for the next batch of biscuits.

When you are ready to bake, preheat the lid and place it atop the Dutch oven. Rake some coals from the fire and place the Dutch oven on them. Then pile some coals on top of the lid. Check the biscuits after 15 minutes. Add more coals on top, if needed. Check every 5 minutes until the rolls are browned on top and bottom. (Also see Camp Dutch Oven, page 43.)

Note: This recipe will make a dozen large biscuits. If your Dutch oven won't hold this many, cook in two batches.

Sourdough French Bread

Most sourdough bread that is baked commercially in San Francisco and other places might be made with an age-old, secret recipe and starter (as advertised), but consistent results are obtained only with the aid of sophisticated baking equipment. Such consistency is difficult to obtain in the home kitchen during changeable weather. On the other hand, making bread exactly the same each time makes it a science rather than an art, and takes some of the excitement out of it.

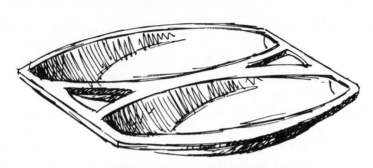

Cast-iron bread pans are available for cooking two perfectly shaped loaves of French bread.

To be honest, sourdough French bread doesn't depend very much on cast iron. True, it can be made in a Dutch oven, but, usually, it is made in a kitchen oven on tin cookie sheets. On the other hand, the heating properties of cast iron are not without value, and a neat bread pan, shaped like two loaves of bread joined together, is still manufactured of cast iron and is, in fact, called a French bread pan. The recipe below will fit it nicely.

2 cups sourdough starter	**1 tablespoon sugar**
4 cups flour	**1 tablespoon cooking oil**
1 cup warm water	**¼ teaspoon salt**
more flour	

Put 4 cups of flour into a bowl. Mix in 1 tablespoon sugar, ¼ teaspoon salt, and 1 tablespoon cooking oil. Make a hole in the center of the mixture and pour in 2 cups of starter and 1 cup of warm water. With a wooden spoon, stir the starter until all of the flour mixture has been taken in. Add a little more flour if you think the dough will take it.

Turn the dough out onto a smooth, well-floured surface. Knead for 10 minutes or longer, adding a little flour as needed to make a smooth, elastic dough. Let the dough rest for 10 minutes. Divide the dough and shape each half into a long, narrow loaf. Grease the cast-iron French bread pan (or a cookie sheet) and place the loaves in it. With a sharp knife, make 45-degree cuts about 1 inch apart along the length of the loaf. Put the bread in a warm spot and let it rise until it doubles in size, which will usually take about an hour and a half.

Preheat the oven to 450 degrees. Bake the bread on a center rack for 15 minutes. Brush the top of each loaf with cold water. Lower the heat to 350 degrees and bake for 20 to 30 minutes, until the crust begins to brown.

I might point out that this recipe, like many other recipes for breads and meats, starts with a high temperature and ends with a lower temperature—which is exactly what happens in an old Dutch oven.

Warning: Sourdough French bread is difficult to make, and you should cook this recipe (or another similar recipe for this bread) several times before inviting guests over to eat it. Be warned, however, that even if you cook it perfectly, some people are not going to appreciate the tough, chewy surface that distinguishes both French and Italian breads. I might add that most French housewives don't normally attempt to bake this bread; instead, they buy it at the bakery. So, be prepared for failure in making this bread, and for hee-haws if you do succeed with it. I like its wonderful flavor, however, and, personally, I've never cooked a loaf that wasn't good at least for dunking in coffee. Except once—and even then my dog, Buff, liked to chew on it.

Sourdough Flapjacks

My recipe for sourdough flapjacks was influenced heavily by *Alaska Magazine's Cabin Cookbook*, which stated, "Hotcakes are about the most popular of all sourdough recipes, and rightly so. If you have any left over they make good sandwiches to take on the trail, and some birds really go for them in a big way when they are broken into pieces."

The recipe below makes a very light flapjack.

½ cup sourdough starter	1 tablespoon sugar
2 cups flour	2 teaspoons baking soda
2 cups warm water	1 teaspoon salt
2 medium chicken eggs	

The night before you are to have flapjacks for breakfast, mix 2 cups of flour and 2 cups of warm water in a glass or crockery container. With a wooden spoon, stir in ½ cup sourdough starter. Cover the container with cheesecloth and put it into a warm place. Let it work overnight. When you are ready to cook, whisk the eggs lightly and stir them into the sponge, along with sugar, baking soda, and salt. Heat the cast-iron griddle and cook immediately. Turn once. Serve with wild honey, butter if you have it, and strong black coffee.

Blueberry Variation: Alaska is noted for wild berries in season, and blueberries are bountiful in some areas. In any case, they are especially good in sourdough pancakes. I make these by merely adding blueberries to the recipe above. But don't mix the blueberries into the batter. Instead, spoon the batter onto the griddle as usual, then quickly add 8 or 10 blueberries on top of the flapjack. Turn and cook the other side. I prefer to serve blueberry pancakes in stacks of three, with butter between each layer, whipped cream on top, and a thick syrup on the side.

Yankee Cooking, Cast-Iron Style

Often we see the terms "cast iron" or "black iron pot" applied to Cajun cooking or southern cooking or Caribbean cooking. Also, during this country's great westward expansion, the Dutch oven and the cast-iron skillet became associated, in the mind's eye, with the rugged life on the frontier and in the great outdoors. Yet, the real cast-iron cookery in this country just might have been perfected at the domestic hearthside back east, where, I presume, more leisure and less concern for bears and Indians permitted the creation of good foodstuffs. The popular image is of the good wife in long dress, apron, and bonnet stooping before a hearth while the man of the house sits back puffing on a long-stemmed clay pipe. Maybe, maybe not. The recipes below show that the Yankee men just might have taken an interest in cooking long before the cast-iron patio grill was invented.

Daniel Webster's Fish Chowder

Arguments will always crop up about what exactly should go into a fish chowder, and whether or not this recipe or that ought to be called New England chowder, Manhattan chowder, or what. When all the thousands of recipes are counted and the day of reckoning comes, here's one that will surely be high on the list. I found it in an old book called *Foods of our Forefathers*, which in turn quoted it from

106 CAST IRON COOKING

the 1931 edition of Suzanne Cary Gruver's *The Cape Cod Cook Book*.

The recipe, said to be suitable for a large fishing party, is in Webster's own words:

"Take a cod of ten pounds, well cleaned, leaving on the skin. Cut into pieces one and a half pounds thick, preserving the head whole. Take one and a half pounds of clear, fat, salt pork, cut in thin slices. Do the same with twelve potatoes. Take the largest pot you have. Try out the pork first; then take out the pieces of pork, leaving the drippings. Add to that three parts of water, a layer of fish, so as to cover the bottom of the pot; next, a layer of potatoes, then two tablespoons of salt, 1 teaspoon of pepper, then the pork, another layer of fish, and the remainder of the potatoes.

"Fill the pot with water to cover the ingredients. Put it over a good fire. Let the chowder boil twenty-five minutes. When this is done, have a quart of boiling milk ready, and ten hard crackers split and dipped in cold water. Add milk and crackers. Let the whole boil five minutes. The chowder is then ready and will be first rate if you have followed the directions. An onion may be added if you like the flavor."

By "try," Webster meant to fry or sauté the salt pork until most of the grease cooks out of it, as when making cracklings. Anyway, be sure to try this old recipe in camp or at home. Webster said to use the largest pot that you have. A large cast-iron Dutch oven will be suitable. Cod has always been a popular fish in New England, but any good fish of mild flavor will be fine.

Nantucket Fireman's Supper

Here's another recipe that came from *The Cape Cod Cook Book*. It called for a spider, which is nothing more than a cast-iron skillet with a long handle and long legs, designed for sliding in and out of a hot bed of coals at the hearth. As a group, firemen still enjoy the reputation of being good cooks, and this recipe indicates that the tradition is quite old. Try it. If you don't have a spider and a hearth, an ordinary cast-iron skillet and a stove eye will do.

pork chops	salt
cooking oil	pepper
onions, peeled and sliced	water
potatoes, peeled and quartered	

Trim the fat off the pork chops. Heat some cooking oil in a spider, or in a skillet if you are cooking on a stovetop. Slowly brown the chops on both sides. Then cover the top of the chops with sliced onions. Add quartered potatoes. Salt and pepper to taste. Add enough water to barely cover the potatoes, bring to heat, cover tightly, and simmer very slowly until the potatoes are tender, about half an hour.

New England Baked Beans

Beans were raised by the Indians and, along with corn, formed a big part of the early American colonial diet. Although there are hundreds of variations on baked bean dishes, often called Boston Baked Beans, here is one that I highly recommend. Most of the Boston recipes seem to call for molasses, which was shipped up from Jamaica for mak-

108 CAST IRON COOKING

ing rum. This recipe from New Hampshire, however, calls for maple syrup and may be closer to Yankee country cooking. I modified the procedure somewhat to make use of a modern oven with thermostat:

1 quart dry beans (try navy
  beans)
½ pound slab of salt pork
½ cup maple syrup
1 medium onion

½ tablespoon salt
½ teaspoon powdered
  mustard
water

Put the beans into a non-metallic container, cover them, and soak them overnight. Drain the beans and put them into a cast-iron pot. Cover with water, bring to boil, and simmer for an hour. Drain the beans.

Preheat the oven to 250 degrees and put on some water to boil. Chop the onion and put it into the bottom of a cast-iron pot of suitable size. Add the beans to the pot. Mix the maple syrup, mustard, and salt, then spread this mixture over the beans. Put the slab of pork on top of the beans so that the rind is up. Cover the beans and pork with boiling water. Bake at 250 degrees for 8 hours. Add a little water from time to time.

Large Batch Cooking

A few weeks ago, I went over to my neighbor's place one night to check on a large batch of turtle soup that had begun to fill the neighborhood with its aroma. My cat also wanted to go. When I got there, Dan Webster, David Herndon, and Tommy Murphy were stirring the pot and boning out 50 pounds of turtle meat, all Florida softshell, some of which had a neck as long as your arm. I stirred the pot myself, noting that it had plenty of tomatoes and onions and okra and other good stuff in with the stock and meat. After tasting of it, I said, joking, that a touch of pepper was what it needed. Before Webster could grab his arm, Murphy dumped in another small box of pepper.

From then on, it was stir, taste, and add. We made several trips to a supermarket and to various kitchens and home freezers for more ingredients. It was, I allow, very good. The recipe? Impossible! By midnight nobody had the slightest idea of what was in that soup. Furthermore, to set forth exact measures here would get Webster, Herndon, or Murphy stirred up at me again, or at each other, with claims that it ought to have more pepper, or less pepper. The truth is that the stir-taste-add method is so much fun that I'm not sure an exact recipe would be advisable, even if I had it. Better, I say, for me to set forth a simple recipe like the Sheep Stew, below, and let the good ol' boys add to it as they go.

Anyhow, the boys entered the turtle soup the next day in a cancer benefit cookoff—and damned if the stuff didn't win first place in the most unusual entry category. A year earlier the same team won the same trophy in the same annual cookoff with a large batch of fried alligator. The gator meat, as I remember, was marinated overnight in a soak (mostly lemon juice) and then seasoned with salt and pepper, coated in flour, and fried as needed at the cookoff (which lasted all the afternoon). They used two gas burner units, topped with fish fryers. Going full blast, these units can cook lots of alligator, chicken, fish, and so on. One problem the team had, however, was that bits of flour accumulated in the bottom of the fryer and burned. If you plan to use such a deep fryer for an extended period, you might rig some sort of wire basket or scoop to clean the bottom from time to time.

In addition to the commercially available "fish fryers," a number of other cast-iron pots and kettles can be used for large-batch cooking. More than once, I've seen fish fried in vats that were made for scalding hogs. But, thinking back on it, all of these events that I have been to were sponsored by some group of peanut farmers, and I suspect that the peanut oil was provided by a local peanut processing company. I would hate to have to *buy* enough oil, at today's prices, to cook in one of these vats!

In any case, remember that large cast-iron pieces should be heated slowly and evenly. It's best to add the oil or water cold, then bring it up to heat gradually.

Sheep Stew

I found this recipe in *The Progressive Farmer's Southern Cookbook*, first published in 1961, but I suspect that the rec-

ipe is much older. It came, the book indicated, from Lunen-
burg County, Virginia, and was used as a fund-raising
event. "Does the school need a piano, library, or new
room?" the text asked. "Think nothing of it. Just announce
a sheep stew. People come to be served and they bring
large containers and buy the surplus. It is amazingly good,
we learned at first hand."

50- to 60-pound fat lamb
3 pounds white fat meat
  (pork)
3 pounds smoked side meat
  (pork)
50 to 60 pounds onions
3 tablespoons red pepper

7 tablespoons black pepper
10 tablespoons salt
4 to 5 pounds butter or
  margarine
3½ to 4 loaves of bread

"Dress lamb and place in refrigerator until thoroughly
chilled. Saw the sides from the backbone and cut the meat
into smaller portions. Place meat in kettle with cold water (a
30- to 35-gallon washpot is good, if you cook it outdoors.)
Start the fire. Add the finely cubed fat meat and side meat,
then add onions. When meat is tender, remove all bones,
and add pepper and salt. If more is needed, add it to suit
the taste. Then add butter or margarine, and bread that has
been broken in small pieces. To stir, use a three- or four-
handled fork.* Be sure to stir enough to keep from sticking
to pot. In adding water while cooking, use hot water. Cook
until thick enough to eat with a fork. This will take 6 hours
or longer. Serve hot. Yield: about 75 servings."

*A pitchfork with 3 or 4 tines.

Burgoo

Traditionally made in large batches, this dish can be cooked with an assortment of meats and vegetables, as indicated by the list below. Just for conversation, I always like to throw in something a little out of the ordinary, such as turtle, along with, maybe, a shoulder of venison, a chunk of beef, lean pork, and a hen or two. Sorry cuts of meat, such as shank, can also be used. Of course, I expect everybody who tries this recipe to improve on it as they go along. Start with:

20 pounds turtle, venison shoulder, beef, or hen
3 gallons cold water
10 bay leaves
½ gallon tomatoes, peeled and diced
4 large onions, chopped
3 ribs celery, chopped, tops and all
6 carrots, chopped
1 quart okra, chopped
1 quart whole kernel corn
2 green peppers, seeded and chopped
1 tablespoon crushed red pepper
3 tablespoons Worcestershire sauce
salt
Tabasco sauce, as needed

Put the cold water and the meats (large chunks) into a small cast-iron wash pot or a kettle. (Before adding the chunks of meat, trim off any fat; and skin the hen.) Build the fire under the pot and bring slowly to boil. (Do not put a cast-iron pot onto a hot wood fire. Fast heating may crack it. It's best to start cold and bring the pot to heat gradually.) Tie the bay leaves in a piece of cloth, or put them into a drawstring tobacco sack, if you've got one empty, and put them into the pot. While the pot is heating, prepare the vegetables. Stir the meat from time to time with a paddle or hickory stick. Cook the meat for an hour or longer. When it is tender, fish out the chunks of meat with a pitch fork. Put the meat aside to drain. Add all the vegetables, pepper, and salt. Bone and chop the meat and add it back to the pot. Discard the bones. Simmer. Stir. Simmer and stir for about 6 hours. Add more water, as needed. Taste the burgoo from time to time and adjust the salt. Add a little Tabasco sauce, as needed for hotness. Half an hour before serving, stir in the Worcestershire sauce. Serve in bowls. Feeds 40 to 60.

Aunt Annie King's Souse

The best souse, or head cheese, that I've ever eaten was made by my Aunt Annie King. She started with a cast-iron washpot, cheese cloth, and the following ingredients.

1 large hog head	½ teaspoon black pepper
1 tablespoon salt	1 medium onion
¼ teaspoon powdered sage	1 cup vinegar
½ teaspoon flaked red pepper	

From the hog head remove the ears, eyes, and brains. Save the brains for scrambling with eggs. Put the rest of the hog head into a cast-iron washpot, under which a good wood fire has been built. If the whole head won't fit into the pot, cut it in half or in quarters. Cover with water and bring to a boil. When the meat is tender and comes from the bones, remove the head from the water and let it cool a bit. (Don't overcook it.) Peel and quarter the onion. Remove the meat from the bones and run it through a food grinder. Run the onion through with the meat. Mix in the vinegar, sage, red pepper, and black pepper.

Shape the mixture into a round ball, which will be about the size of a grapefruit, and wrap it in a square of cheesecloth of suitable dimension. (A piece of old sheet will also work.) Wrap and twist the cloth, putting pressure on the ball of souse. Tie off tightly and hang in a cool place for at least 12 hours. Or longer. (Waiting can be the hard part.) Be sure to put a container under the ball to catch any grease that drips out. Slice the souse and serve it with crackers. It's best at room temperature, but it can be refrigerated and kept for a week or so.

Many cookbook writers tell you to put all manner of stuff into head cheese, such as lemon zest and coriander. Even cinnamon. Suit yourself.

When cleaning the hog's head for making souse, some people include the ears. After cooking, the ears can be cut up and used, but the pieces end up being somewhat chewy and, being of a different color than the rest of the mixture, they tend to stand out. I recommend that you omit the ears from your first batch of souse.

Many people also include the pig's feet when they make up a batch of souse, partly because, I suppose, they don't know what else to do with them. There are various recipes for "trotters," as pig's feet are called, and many people like them pickled. I allow that they are tolerable if properly prepared. But a character in the *Foxfire* books had the best solution. After butchering hogs, he would package the feet in a shoe box and mail them to a friend who professed to love them.

Other Cast-Iron Pieces

Although the skillet and the Dutch oven are by far the most popular cast-iron pieces found in the modern kitchen, a number of other items are still manufactured and are quite useful. Some of these old pieces are discussed below, along with some newcomers, such as cast-iron woks and ribbed griddles.

PIE IRONS

Pie irons consist of two very small skillet-shaped pieces. Designed for open-fire cooking, the two skillets hinge together and have long handles. You can put pie dough in one unit, add apple pie mix or other suitable filling, top with another piece of dough, close the irons, cook on one side, turn the irons over, cook on the other side, open—and you've got apple turnovers. Although pie irons can still be used successfully for cooking pies, the main use for modern man is in preparing sandwiches and light meals.

I've got two pie irons. One is square, designed to hold two pieces of ordinary loaf bread. The other is round, designed to hold the two halves of a hamburger bun or an English muffin. I sometimes use my pie irons at my kitchen hearth, and they come in handy in a camping situation where you need to cook over an open fire but don't have time to wait for coals to burn down for ideal cooking. By closing the two lids, you can cook directly in the flames.

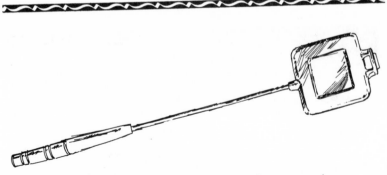

Long handled pie irons, hinged together, are great for cooking small portions over a campfire.

You can use either half of the pie iron as a mini skillet, just large enough to cook an egg or pan fry a small trout that has been cut in half, or maybe for grilling a couple of pieces of fresh venison tenderloin in a deer camp. Frankly, however, long handled pie irons are a little awkward to take on a camping trip if you are traveling light.

I've cooked a couple of small meat pies on my pie irons, and I've made even more hot sandwiches, such as the reuben. My favorite, however, is a grilled steak made with a fillet of beef tenderloin. Warm the pie irons. Add butter to one half of the pie iron. Center a few rounds from a slice of onion. Sprinkle a little salt and pepper on the steak and center it over the onion slices. Place a little butter on top, then close the pie irons. Put directly on hot coals and cook for 4 minutes on each side.

CAST-IRON MUFFIN PANS

Cast-iron muffin pans are still being manufactured, along with related pans for cooking popovers and Danish cakes. Any good family-type cookbook has plenty of muffin recipes, but here's an old one that I would like to pass along. Although this recipe calls for huckleberries, you can also use blueberries and other small fruit or chopped fruit.

2 cups all-purpose flour	3 tablespoons lard
¾ cup huckleberries	3 tablespoons sugar
1 chicken egg	3 teaspoons baking powder
1 cup milk	½ teaspoon salt

If the milk, egg, and other ingredients are in the refrigerator, set them out until they reach room temperature. Preheat the oven to 425 degrees. Grease the cast-iron muffin pan. Sift together the flour, sugar, baking powder, and salt. In a bowl, beat the chicken egg and whisk in the milk and lard. Add the flour mixture and huckleberries to the bowl and stir. Fill each cavity in the muffin pan two-thirds full. Bake for 25 to 30 minutes, or until the top of the muffins are lightly browned.

Also try any good muffin recipe or commercial mix in cast-iron pans. And remember that biscuits and cornbreads can be cooked in a muffin pan. And try your favorite reci-

Even Aebleskiever pans are available in cast iron.
These can also be used for ordinary muffins.

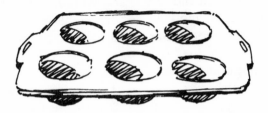

Cast-iron muffin pans are available in several sizes and shapes.

pes for popovers or aebleskievers—unless, of course, you've got a separate aebleskiever pan made of cast iron.

Nothing bakes better than cast iron. Try muffins made in our pans and you'll never use a flimsy muffin tin again.
—Century Cast-Iron Cookware

FLUTED CAKE PAN

The German bundt cake, a sort of pound cake with a topping, is cooked in a circular fluted pan with a solid center. Such a cast-iron pan is also ideal for cooking other cakes, plain and fancy, of the same shape. The pan can also be used for baking breads.

BREAD STICKS AND PANS

The familiar bread sticks, some of which are shaped like half an ear of corn, are always popular, and, of course, cast-iron pans to make them are still available. Also, a pan that makes pie-shaped pieces of bread is manufactured in two sizes. All of these pans are used primarily for corn breads.

My nephew, David Livingston, uses cast-iron corn stick pans to mold lead into convenient units. With the lead he makes fishing lure components, mostly spinnerbaits and buzz bait heads. He buys bulk lead alloy by the ton, and it comes in 65-pound pigs. The 65-pound pigs are melted in a cast-iron pot, then the molten lead is dipped out, with a cast-iron ladle, and poured into cast-iron corn stick pans. Each "stick" weighs a pound, give or take an ounce or two.

Pans for baking "corn stick" pieces of bread
have always been popular.

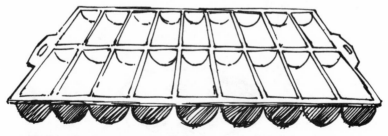

Nothing beats cast-iron for cooking cornbread, and a number of
special bread pans are available.

These sticks of lead are an ideal size and shape to use in 20-pound lead pots made for pouring lead into small molds.

David also makes his own lure molds. First, he melts aluminum in a cast-iron pot, then sand casts the aluminum into roughly shaped molds. Then he has to finish the molds by hand, using dental tools.

Melting lead and other metal in cast iron is an old tradition, and a small melting pot (4½ inches in diameter) is still manufactured. It has a handle and a pouring lip. Comes in handy for keeping barbecue sauce on a grill, too.

CAST-IRON WOKS

Some of the best woks are made in China. Usually, they are fabricated from a flat piece of iron that is hammered down into a mold. It is therefore a more malleable iron that true cast iron. On the other hand, true cast iron probably originated in China some 2500 years ago, and it was no doubt used for cooking purposes even then. In any case, Lodge Manufacturing has recently introduced a cast-iron wok, and it is truly great. Successful wok cooking depends on having

Cast iron is a good material for wok cooking because it heats evenly and withstands very high temperatures.

a high heat source in the bottom of the utensil, for which cast iron is just perfect.

There are several good wok books on the market, and I won't offer recipes here. I would, however, like to borrow a text on stir-frying from a brochure from Lodge manufacturing and House of Tsang:

"The curved shape of a wok produces graduated temperature zones which allow you to cook many different ingredients without having to remove them from the wok. The bottom of the wok next to the flame is very hot and can be used for searing and sealing. Push food up along the sloping side walls of the wok to keep it warm. This gives you room to stir-fry other ingredients."

Some of the Teflon-coated woks on the market won't hold up to high heat, and are too slick, really, to hold the food up the sides. In this respect, the hammered Chinese wrought iron version may be better than cast iron. I should hasten to add that the cast-iron wok is "textured," meaning that it is cast in rather rough sand. In any case, the Lodge wok is made with a convenient handle on one side and a lifting grip on the other.

DEEP FRYERS

Although I am partial to a good skillet, for the reasons set forth under the section on frying chicken and fish, I allow that some purely excellent cast-iron deep fryers are on the market. These range in size and configuration, depending partly on how they are to be heated. One oblong unit, for example, works best on a grill or grid. Round units work best on stove eyes. The illustrations show some of the more popular models.

Frying was covered earlier in this book, but I want to

*Some round deep fryers come with baskets
for holding French fries, fish, or chicken.*

*Large cast-iron fryers, oblong shaped, work nicely over two stove
eyes or on a camp stove. Some of these fryers have a lid that can
also be used as a griddle.*

*Lids for cookware are available in cast iron
as well as glass and plastic.*

point out here that these cast-iron pieces can be used for other purposes. A 9-by-17-inch "camp fryer," for example, is an excellent piece for baking a large batch of cornbread in the kitchen oven.

CAST-IRON KETTLES

Kettles, with a pouring spout, came in handy for heating and pouring water back when most of the cooking was accomplished at a hearth or on a wood stove. A cast-iron model is still available and is great for making instant coffee or heating water for tea, but of course our modern hot water heaters and indoor plumbing reduces the importance of kettles for cooking and bathing.

Another cast-iron piece, called a Country Kettle, is used primarily for serving stews and such. It holds only a pint, and has little legs on it. This limits its use as a cooking utensil.

FAJITA GRIDDLES & SIZZLEWARE

I've got what is called a fajita griddle, and I use it for flapjacks, fried eggs, tortillas, pizzas, and other good things. But I'll have to admit that I'm more than a little confused about the term "fajita"—and how to make the real thing. One point is pretty clear: tortillas are required, often made of flour, and a griddle is ideal for this purpose, as pointed out in the section on Mexican cooking. The rest of the fajita consists of meat, tomatoes, onions, and other fillings, all of

More and more, cast iron is being used for serving as well as for cooking. Some griddles come with wooden or rattan underliners.

which are placed in the center of a warm tortilla and rolled up. Beyond that I hesitate to go, but I will add that some people in Texas refer to the fajita as a Mexican hotdog.

One manufacturer markets what they call sizzleware (Lodge Texas Fajita Sizzleware) and poops it up as a heated serving platter. They also market round and oval "underliners" made of solid wood or rattan, which, of course, prevent the hot cast-iron platter from burning the table or tablecloth. This line of cast iron comes in various sizes and shapes, including a crescent-shaped serving piece. In other words, the main function of sizzleware is in serving the food, not in cooking it. But, of course, some of the pieces can also be used for cooking.

The trick in sizzleware is to preheat the oven to 350 degrees and put the griddle (cast-iron platter) into it for 30 minutes. Then grill the meat or broil it. (If you broil it in the oven, merely switch the heat from broil to bake. Broil the meat on a separate rack, usually very close to the heat source, and leave the griddle on a separate rack down under the meat.) When the meat is done, put it onto the heated griddle and place it on an "underliner" on the table. Have hot tortillas, chopped tomatoes, and other fajita mak-

ings. I tried the method, and find that the cast iron on the
table does add a touch of the quaint.

DOUBLE SKILLETS

A double unit features a griddle that fits perfectly atop a
deeper skillet. Either piece may be used separately, or the
griddle can be used as a cover. This is, of course, a neat unit
for cooking in camp. In addition to being quite versatile, it's
great for making smother-fried squirrel and similar dishes
that require both frying and steaming. Here's the recipe for
tough squirrels, which, I guess, goes back to my grand-
father.

In this double unit, a shallow skillet fits atop a pot.
They can be used together or separately.

Smother-Fried Squirrel

3 gray squirrels or 2 fox
  squirrels
buttermilk
cooking oil
flour
1 medium onion, chopped
salt

black pepper
1 tablespoon Worcestershire
  sauce
water
beef bouillon cube
rice or biscuits (cooked
  separately)

Skin the squirrels and cut them into serving sized pieces. Put the pieces in a glass container and cover them with buttermilk. Refrigerate the squirrel for 6 hours, or, better, overnight. When you are ready to cook, heat a cup of water and melt the bouillon cube in it. Drain the squirrels, salt and pepper each piece, and roll in flour. Heat some peanut oil in the deeper skillet and brown the squirrel. Pour off most of the grease and pour in the water with bouillon. Bring to low boil, reduce heat to very low, and simmer.

Add 2 tablespoons of oil in the shallow skillet. Sauté the onions for a minute or two, then slowly stir in 2 tablespoons of flour and Worcestershire sauce. Simmer for ten minutes, stirring constantly. Remove from heat if the onions tend to brown. Add a cup of water and stir while shaking the pan. Pour flour and water mixture from the shallow skillet over the squirrel pieces in the deeper skillet. Cover tightly and cook on very low heat for an hour or two. Add more water from time to time if needed. About 20 minutes before you're ready to eat, sprinkle on some freshly ground black pepper. Transfer the pieces from the skillet directly to serving plates. Spoon gravy over rice or hot biscuits.

Company Variation: Cut back on the last application of

black pepper and sprinkle the meat pieces with parsley. Put the gravy into a small serving bowl and forbid sopping at the table.

Camp Variation: The above recipe can easily be cooked in camp, and is perfect for double skillets and a two-burner gas stove. In camp, omit everything except squirrel, oil, onion, flour, salt, pepper, and water. Try bacon drippings if you don't have cooking oil at hand.

EGG & BACON SKILLET

I'm happy to report that a skillet is made especially for cooking breakfast. It's square—and just the right dimension for bacon. Further, it has a ridge through the middle, separating the bacon side from the egg side. And the egg side is also divided. Thus, it is perfect for cooking four pieces of bacon and two fried eggs.

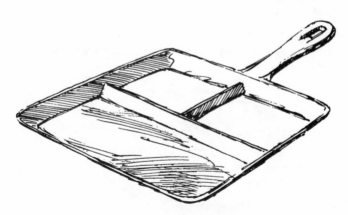

A convenient cast-iron breakfast skillet will hold two eggs and four slices of bacon.

THE JUMBO SKILLET

A 20-inch cast-iron skillet was recently introduced for cooking at family reunions and other such gatherings. It holds over 3 gallons of oil. Unlike other skillets, it doesn't have a one-handed handle and pouring spouts. Rather, it is perfectly round and has short lifting handles on either side. This is a highly specialized piece. It will, to be sure, turn out lots of hamburgers, flapjacks, fried fish, and so on; but it is a difficult skillet to heat on stove eyes. Having no handle, it is difficult to put on and take off of a camp fire; most skillets, by comparison, can be lifted off the fire or coals with a handle. On the other hand, this skillet will work nicely on some of the new portable stoves that burn bottled gas.

RIBBED GRIDDLES AND SKILLETS

In his recipe for pan steak, as discussed earlier in this book, George Herter claimed that many famous restaurants fried

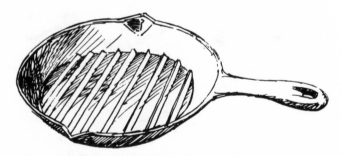

Ribbed cast-iron skillets are used for stove-top broiling.

steaks for customers, then made grid marks on them with a heated rod in order to keep the customers happy! Now they can use a ribbed skillet or griddle. These are manufactured especially for pan "broiling" and are, I point out, not much good for frying an egg or cooking a flapjack. So don't buy one for its versatility. These units are also said to be good for "grease-free frying." Frankly, I don't know quite what they are talking about, and I suspect that some advertising copy writer is either being downright dishonest or is flirting with an oxymoron.

I've got a ribbed griddle, however, and I do like to use it from time to time for cooking strips of bacon and slabs of cured ham.

CHEF'S SKILLET

This neat piece, about 10 inches in diameter, has more slope to the sides than regular skillets have, and the handle has a more comfortable arch for chefs who like to shake instead of stir. The skillet is ideal for sautéing a few onions, for making sauces, and so on. It can also be used to stir-fry food,

The chef's skillet has sloping sides and a comfortable handle.

and is hereby recommended to those aces who desire to flip a patty of hash browns into the air and catch it, turned and intact, on the way down.

LARGE GRIDDLES

Several large griddles are manufactured. Some are round, designed for cooking over gas burners, and others are rectangular. Some are made to double as lids for large deep fryers, and these, usually oval in shape, are great for camp use. Some of these units are made especially to fit outdoor cookers.

Some of the larger rectangular griddles work nicely on a two-burner gas stove, and can be used at home on electric ranges. I like to use one for cooking breakfast when no definite serving time has been set. The trick, of course, is to put the large griddle over two stove eyes, one turned up to medium heat and one to warm. Cook on the hotter end and, with a spatula, move the bacon, sausage, eggs, and flapjacks down to the other end when they are done. A single

Large griddles are available for cooking over two stove eyes,
or for cooking on a camp stove.
The one shown here drains off surplus grease.

cook with one of these rectangular griddles can feed lots of people, especially if they serve their own plates.

My rectangular griddle measures 11 by 19 inches. It looks flat, but it is actually sloped so that excess oil drains to the perimeter. It also has a well in one corner for holding excess bacon grease. It is a joy to use this unit—provided that the stove is level.

SMALL FRY GRIDDLE

Century Cast-Iron Cookware markets a tiny griddle, 5 inches square, that is ideal for making grilled cheese sandwiches. It also comes in handy for camping trips, and for blackening small steaks or chops.

HIBACHI GRILLS AND CAST-IRON GRIDS

A lot of Hibachi-type grills are imported. Some are good, and some are not so good. There are a couple of heavy-duty

Some of the best Hibachi-style grills are made of cast iron.

cast-iron models made in America, and I am fond of using these. The better ones have adjustable dampers, giving you some control of your heat. Although they are usually used along with charcoal, I am guilty of using coals from my fire in a Hibachi, and I'll sometimes build a fire from small pieces of green pecan or hickory wood. Coal also makes a very good fuel for Hibachi cooking, if you can find it these days. Of course, the Hibachi can also be used on the patio, in camp, or on the tailgate.

I would also like to point out that cast-iron grids are available for outdoor cooking units. These are heavy duty grids, available in several sizes, and come complete with a handy grid lifter. If seasoned properly, a cast-iron grid cooks nicely, doesn't stick, and lasts for many years. I use a large cast-iron grid atop ordinary bricks to grill chicken and steaks and kabobs in my kitchen fireplace. Such grids can also be used for building your own outdoor cooking units, and for camping.

CAST-IRON TRIVET AND MEAT RACK

I've got an 8-inch cast-iron piece that can be used as a trivet or as a meat rack in a Dutch oven. It's perfect. It is round, with round holes for ventilation, and has short legs. Years ago, a long-legged model was designed to sit over a bed of coals.

THE BACON PRESS

Dried blackeyed peas and ham hocks are often cooked on New Year's day. This dish, a custom in some parts of the

A cast-iron trivet comes in mighty handy from time to time, and it can also be used as a rack in a dutch oven or other pot.

country, is said to bring good luck. But I know some folks who claim that salt pork must be used, and some even narrow it down to salt-cured hog jowls. Frankly, I don't really care for hog jowls cooked in this manner. I prefer mine cured, smoked, and sliced like bacon. (I don't have nationwide figures, but in my neck of the woods smoke-cured hog jowls, sliced, sells for about half the price of smoke cured bacon.) The trouble is that the jowl has a natural curve, and it is almost impossible to fry strips of it like bacon. It curls up. If you've got a bacon press, however, you're in business.

Hog Jowls and Chicken Eggs

smoked hog jowls
chicken eggs
salt and pepper

biscuits or toast (cooked
    separately)
fresh tomatoes

Heat the skillet and arrange strips of hog jowl in it. Cover with bacon press and cook until bottom is browned. Turn, cover with bacon press, and cook until the other side is done. (If necessary to prevent overlapping, cook the hog jowl slices in more than one batch.) Remove the meat and put it on absorbent paper to drain. Pour off the grease. Fry the eggs in the skillet. I prefer mine flipped over, but not well done. Suit yourself. Salt and pepper the eggs to taste and serve with hog jowl strips, biscuits or toast, and sliced tomatoes.

The bacon press, I might add, also does a good job of keeping your bacon straight when you cook it in a skillet or on a griddle. Every man needs one.

LIDS FOR CAST-IRON COOKWARE

Cast-iron cookware is usually sold with either cast-iron lids or glass lids. Glass lids usually have a knob on top for handling, whereas cast iron has a suitcase-type handle, arched. Either kind is usually dome shaped, which is an excellent design for using on a stove, where coals will not be piled on top of the lid. Most of the modern lids are called self-basting, which means that moisture from the food condenses on the dome lid, forms droplets of water, and drips down on the food. The underside of some of these lids have a number of protuberances from which the droplets fall.

The disadvantage of glass, of course, is that it breaks easily. The disadvantages of cast iron are (1) you can't see through it, (2) it is heavy, (3) it costs almost as much as the pan itself, and (4) it can disflavor dishes during long cooking periods if it is not seasoned properly. Still, I'll take cast iron every time.

More and more we are seeing plastic lids in cookware retail outlets, no doubt because of the high price of good glass lids or cast-iron lids. While the plastic may be all right for some applications, I much prefer a heavy lid for long, slow cooking, simply because the weight keeps it seated more firmly. In a pinch, metal lids, such as aluminum or tin, can also be used on cast-iron pieces, if they fit.

The better manufacturers of cast-iron products market lids separately for their cookware, and these can be purchased separately in case you lose or break a lid. But these days many retailers balk at special orders, and some simply will not provide this service. Some independent dealers may order the pieces for you, but, considering their time and high shipping costs for a small order, it is understandable if they utter a strong word or two when you tell them that you bought the original piece from a discount store.

CAST-IRON LIDS FOR CAMP DUTCH OVENS

A camp oven should have a cast-iron lid, not a glass lid. Of course, the handle is in the middle of the lid, and it should be in the form of an arch. Remember that the handle will often be covered up with coals, and that it must be removed with a hook of some sort. Getting the hook in the exact center of the handle, and thereby in the center of the lid, is very important. If the lid tilts when you take it off, ashes may fall into the food. Thus, it should be lifted straight up, and with the hook in the dead center of the lid. To this end, the handle should have a notch centered on the underside. If the lid to your Dutch oven doesn't have a suitable notch, purchase a triangular file and make one.

Also, remember that the lid of a Dutch oven should fit very tightly, especially if the oven is to be left unattended for long periods of time. If the lid doesn't fit tightly, too much moisture gets away and the food could burn. Some lids fit well, and others don't. Your best bet is to follow a tip from an article in the April 1971 issue of *Field & Stream* by Ted Trueblood: "If the lid of a new oven doesn't seat well, smear valve-grinding compound on the rim of the pot and the edge of the lid and rotate it until you have a fit like a bank vault door." Be warned, however, that this is a slow process. But it's well worth the effort, if your lid doesn't seat properly. If you aren't familiar with valve-grinding compound, check with your auto parts retail outlet.

Another trick that will help a loose lid, at least temporarily, is to make a paste of flour and water. After the Dutch oven has been loaded with food, coat the edge of the lid and rim of the Dutch oven with the flour paste. Seat the lid, and leave it be for the duration of the cooking period. If you take a peak, the seal will be broken.

CAMP OVEN LID HOOKS

A one-armed man fitted with a good hook can lift a camp Dutch oven lid niftily, but the rest of us need some sort of hook on a handle. Commercial Dutch oven tools, both long and short, are available, or you can make your own by screwing a suitable hook into the end of a wooden handle. The lid hook can also be used to lower a Dutch oven by the bail into a pit of hot coals, or to remove it from the pit. The commercial tools also have a cross piece that is useful for raking hot coals around.

STOVE-TOP DUTCH OVEN LIDS

Lids for stove-top Dutch ovens aren't quite as important as for the camp models, simply because they merely cover the pot and never hold coals for heating and cooking purposes. For this reason, they usually have dome-shaped lids. Some of these can be purchased with either glass or cast-iron lids. I prefer self-basting cast iron, but good heatproof glass lids do work very well.

SKILLET LIDS

Remember that most cast-iron skillets are manufactured with a pour spout on either side, and a normal lid will not cover this entirely. Special lids are available for cast-iron skillets, but they are expensive and are seldom available in most retail outlets. Usually, lids are not needed for skillet cooking, although there are, of course, exceptions.

Smother-fried meats, for example, work best with a lid, and, under some conditions a lid is highly desirable for cooking in camp. So, you may want to shop around for a cast-iron skillet with a special lid.

OTHER LIDS

Lids for such cast-iron pieces as bean pots should fit tightly, especially when food is cooked unattended for long periods of time. Most of the round pots come with lids, or the lids can be purchased separately. Or lids made for other pots may work satisfactorily, either in glass or other material.

Some large cast-iron pieces, such as rectangular fish cookers, often come with lids. Before buying one of these pieces, look around for one that comes with a lid that also serves as a large griddle.

Appendix

HOW CAST-IRON POTS ARE MADE

Lowell Branham, Outdoors Editor of the *Knoxville News-Sentinel*, made a tour of a cast-iron factory in 1988, and here is part of his report:

"The heart of the manufacturing operation is a huge furnace where raw iron is heated to a temperature of 2,800 degrees. At that point, it glows a brilliant yellow orange and flows almost as freely as water.

"The molten iron travels from the furnace to various production points in huge steel pots. To create a cast-iron vessel, the molten metal is poured from the pot into a mold of sand.

"The sand molds are what give cast-iron cookware its characteristic grainy surface. When the metal has solidified and cooled in the mold, the sand is broken away and recycled.

"Pieces coming from the molds are covered with a crust of sand particles that have fused to the metal. To remove the crust, the pieces are sent to a blasting machine and bombarded with fine steel shot.

"A workman then inspects each piece and grinds away any rough edges left from the molding process. From there, the pieces go into a media bath that burnishes away their sandpaper-like roughness and leaves a smooth grain that's pleasing to the touch. As a final step, the pieces are dipped in a wax bath to prevent rusting and then transported to the warehouse area to await shipment."

Some cast-iron pieces are left with a rather rough cooking surface, and others are polished, or machined, to a smoother finish. If I have a choice, I prefer a slick surface for cooking bacon and eggs, but a rough surface works nicely for bread pans and for frying chicken and fish.

MANUFACTURERS OF CAST-IRON COOKWARE

Century Cookware, P.O. Box 2647, Birmingham, AL 35202. This firm, established in 1902, is a branch of the Birmingham Stove Company and now specializes in cast-iron products. They offer a large line of cookware for home or camp, including camp Dutch ovens. Write for a brochure.

Lodge Manufacturing Company, P.O. Box 380, South Pittsburg, TN 37380. This old firm in the Appalachians started making cast-iron cookware in 1896, when William McKinley was President, and is still family owned and operated. Lodge is the country's largest manufacturer of cast-iron cookware. Write for a brochure.

Rome Industries, Inc., 1703 West Detweiller Drive, Peoria, IL 61615. Rome manufactures a number of interesting items for outdoor and campfire cookery, but most of it, being aluminum, is not in tune with the spirit of this book. They do, however, have cast-iron pie irons that come in handy at the hearth or by campfire.

Durango Cookery, P.O. Box 2137, Durango, CO 81302. The products marketed by Durango are intended for outdoor use, either on the patio or in camp, and most of them are made of aluminum. They make a bottled gas cooker, and they do have a 14-inch cast-iron skillet and an 18-inch cast-iron griddle for the system.

Wagner's General Housewares Corp., Terre Haute, IN 47804. I've seen several cast-iron pieces, including a fajita pan, that were manufactured by this firm. But their current line seems to be rather limited, and, if my information is complete, they sell primarily through department stores.

ANTIQUE PIECES

Cast iron will last for centuries, and even very old pieces can still be used for cooking. Antiques shops, junk shops, flea markets, and old houses or barns are the most likely places to look for old cast iron. Although antique skillets and Dutch ovens can still be used, the only pieces mentioned below are those that are no longer manufactured. I'm no expert on antiques, and I offer no advice on dating such pieces. But I suspect that the expert can place cast iron ware pretty closely, and the old stuff is different from the modern. It has a different look about it, a different feel to it. For example, I recently saw some cast-iron pieces hanging on the wall at Choctawhatchee Lodge, and two of the skillets had a ring on the underside. In other words, if they were put on a modern kitchen stove, only the outer ring would touch the stove eye. They were, of course, made for cooking on a wood-burning stove with removeable eyes.

In any case, anyone who has an interest in antiques as such will be able to find additional information in any good library. Although my brother, Colonel Ira L. Livingston, is something of an expert on old stuff, I confess that I haven't made even a literary search of such pieces. But I will say that my interest in cast-iron cooking has made my visits to antiques stores and junk shops (usually at the instigation of some woman) more enjoyable. Sometimes, while driving down the highway, I even have an urge to wheel into such a wayside junk shop.

WAFFLE IRONS

To be sure, waffle irons are still widely used, but most of the ones available today are not cast iron and are made with internal electrical heating elements. The older waffle irons, hinged, were designed for heating over flames or coals. When hot, the irons were removed from the fire and opened. The waffle batter was poured into the proper cavity, and the hinged unit sides were shut. The hot cast iron cooked the waffle, without the unit being over the fire. In fact, the expert could cook two waffles before having to re-heat the cast iron.

Typically, antique waffle irons will have very long handles.

TOASTERS

Cast iron pieces of various designs were used for toasting bread at the hearthside. Usually, these were upright pieces which sat on legs and held slices of bread vertically to catch the radiant heat. Most of these had a swivel mechanism, which permitted the browning of first one side and then the other.

SPIDERS

Early housewives had spider skillets that were designed especially for cooking on a hearth. They had long legs, for sitting over a bed of coals, and long handles. They were great for hearthside cooking, but would be almost useless on a modern kitchen stove. Nor are they ideal for a campfire, since the legs work best for sliding across a flat surface.

TRIVETS

These long-legged pieces were designed for holding a pot or other hot item on the hearth. They were also used to keep pots and pans directly over coals without touching them.

ANDIRONS

Although modern andirons aren't made with the cook in mind, some of the old ones had built-in hooks for holding spits. If you like to cook in a kitchen fireplace, as I do, keep an eye out for a set. They are sometimes called firedogs.

OYSTER ROASTERS

Similar in concept to waffle irons, hinged oyster roasters have star-shaped sides for holding six oysters. Anyone who has roasted oysters on a piece of tin or over a grill will appreciate the design. The idea, of course, is to hold the fresh oyster over the heat until the shell opens. Then the oysters are served, hot, on the half shell. Roasting too long will dry out the oysters, taking away their flavor and texture. Only fresh, unshelled oysters should be used for roasting. In any case, this delicacy has almost disappeared from the American scene, and the old cast-iron roasters are things of the past. What a pity.